Building Faith
Through A Carpenter's Hands
Brandon Russell with Danielle A. Vann

WALDORF PUBLISHING

Published by Waldorf Publishing
2140 Hall Johnson Road
#102-345
Grapevine, Texas 76051
www.WaldorfPublishing.com

Building Faith Through A Carpenter's Hands

ISBN: 978-1-943848-58-4
Library of Congress Control Number: 2015957015
Copyright © 2016

Front Photo Credit: Jennifer Hancock

Praise for *Building Faith Through A Carpenter's Hands*

"Owning a hammer and saw makes no man a carpenter. What Brandon possesses greater than his toolset is the mindset and skill set of a humble craftsman. His story of becoming a master of both his trade and character is an inspiration to readers who also seek to build from God's plans for their life." **Jonathan Catherman**, **Author of International bestseller *The MANUAL TO MANHOOD***

"Brandon was more than a friend to me. He was my mentor, role model, and a real brother in Christ. Brandon found me in the gym one day and saw a young kid who knew absolutely nothing about lifting weights or living a clean lifestyle. As we started training together on a daily basis, I saw how Brandon treated his body as God's Temple and what it meant to live a Christian lifestyle. Over the years that followed, our friendship matured into a brotherhood of Christ." **Yaakov Baum, Police Officer for the City of Dunwoody, Georgia**

"I've had the pleasure to witness and accompany Brandon through significant parts of his winding journey, and watched him accumulate his hearty collection of valuable "tools in his toolbox." His unshakeable faith, incredible resiliency, and motivational inspiration are a true testimony to the power of God's ability and love." **Lauren Makk, Celebrity Designer, Television Host, Owner & Senior Designer of Lauren Makk Interiors**

"Brandon has always been that guy that stands out in a positive light in everything he does. He is an invaluable resource for anyone who wants to model themselves after a person who always takes the high road. Brandon has maintained integrity and faith throughout all his years of modeling. In our business, this is a rare and unique point of view." **Ed Locke, owner, Locke Models**

"If you ever need anything, I'm here for you." One year later, on the verge of suicide, I faintly recalled this sincere offer. I called him up and was met with a grace that changed my life forever. **Parker Wade**

"My first meeting with Brandon happened while working on Trading Spaces. I was impressed by his enthusiasm, work ethic, and his carpentry skills. As I worked with him, I realized he had a true Christian ethic. That ethic was evident in his willingness to help people with their problems. This could have been involving home repair issues or "life issues." Since then, and through many conversations, my opinion and respect for Brandon have just grown." **Frank Bielec, Children's Book Author and Celebrity Designer for the Television Series, Trading Spaces**

Dedication

I dedicate this book to the two founders of my foundation. My father, Dennis Russell, and my mother, Martha Jo Russell. Without having been equally poured into by these amazing examples of truth, character, love, faith, and the belief in building the true purpose and calling God created me for, I would not be able to stand on the solid foundation of faith I have built upon today. I love you for all you have given me and I hope to have served you proudly in all that I have and continue to accomplish in life.

Love,
Brandon

Table of Contents

Table of Contents for Tools in the Toolbox

Psalm 19:14

[14] May these words of my mouth and this meditation of my heart be pleasing in your sight, LORD, my Rock and my Redeemer.

Chapter 1
What's in Your Toolbox?

How solid is your foundation? Not the one your home sits on, but the foundation in which you rest your life and your spirituality. It's an intriguing question, isn't it?

It's certainly one worth exploring.

My personal foundation in faith started at a young age. From the moment I knew there was a God, I believed. I've marked myself as a follower of the word, a card-carrying member of God's army if you will. While this view may not be popular with some, I undoubtedly know my feet stand on a rock-solid foundation. That unshakeable ground didn't come without a struggle or two … three … or four … or fifteen; okay, you get what I mean; I've struggled, and for that matter still do, I'm human!

When I was given the remarkable opportunity to write **Building Faith Through A Carpenter's Hands**, I was met with a host of challenges. How could I encourage you, the reader, to come to know me as more than just a celebrity carpenter from a television show that revolutionized the world of D-I-Y (Do-It-Yourself)? More importantly, how could I relate and invoke my passion and fire for Christ on a five-by-eight page? What tools of wisdom could I pull from my spiritual toolbox and lend to you? Bottom line: *What in the world would this book be about*?

As you will soon learn, I'm a firm believer in walking the walk and the old adage "actions speak louder than words." If someone has to tell you they are a Christian then the examples they are putting forth in the world are not doing a good enough job showing their faith. It's a hard subject for me. One I knew I would be grappling with when the pencil met the paper. Don't get me wrong, I love to share my faith with anyone who is willing to listen, what I do not like to do is push without an invitation.

Still, I am who I am. I'm a believer. To write a book about my life without a healthy dose of faith is simply not possible. One of my favorite questions I'm asked is: Are you a Christian? My response is always the same. Are you ready for the answer? Here it is: *"No, I am **the** church."* It's an answer I will explain throughout the book and one that will surely have you looking at faith in a new way.

The struggle of knowing what to say and how to say it turned over in my mind for a great deal of time. How do I lead by example and still communicate how fallible I am in life and in the very faith I've been asked to address. I did what I always do when seeking a significant answer; I turned to prayer and conversation. I took the time to *listen* to God. I took the time to do a fair amount of soul-searching. As God always seems to do, he provided a sudden stroke of purpose that made me realize that this book was placed in my path to be as much of a walk through my own journey to spirituality as it has been designed to help you gather a solid set of spiritual tools of your own.

When God calls you to share his word and the tools he has blessed you with, the best thing one can do is answer the call. That is in no way to say that I have all the answers, nor will I ever claim that I do.

Yet that may leave you asking yourself: What credentials do I possess that give me the ability to impart these proclaimed words of wisdom? To tell you the truth, I'm just a southern boy who's been blessed to have learned a thing or two through some pretty extraordinary experiences.

When I say extraordinary, I am not only alluding to the events that earned the word "celebrity" before my name. To only share those moments is an injustice to the person I truly am—both on and off the camera. You see, at age forty, I look back and realize my days traveling the world as a model, my time on a groundbreaking television show, and the work I've done inside people's homes and even God's house, have granted me an insight that some only gain when they have reached twice my age.

While others may look at my life and see it as different from their own, let me assure you that at the core, it's not. In fact, I would be willing to bet my struggles mirror some of your own.

I've failed. I've failed more times than I would care to admit.

I've struggled and refused to surrender at times.

I've given into my will and not God's.

I've messed up a time or two. I've been unkind when it wasn't my intention. I've been hard on others and myself. Sadly, I've given into selfish pride.

I've worked hard and had it all disappear when I wasn't ready to let it go.

Any of these sound familiar? No matter what your age, having a struggle to bear is what levels the playing field of humanity. At times, we are forced to face incredible storms—hard-earned life lessons disguised as troubles. It's the moments when the bottom drops out, and the world is suddenly upside down. It's in these small fragments of time that you have to ask yourself, "Will this break me or do I have the strength to pull myself up and carry on?"

If you haven't had the pleasure, yes, I said pleasure, of these uncomfortable moments where God calls you out and puts you to the test, don't worry; they will come. It's part of our mission here on earth—to grow, to weather the ups and downs, to gain a deeper perspective, and build a strong foundation within Him. God has a way of getting us down to ground level so he can whisper a new beginning in our ear. Even though these times often come filled with pain, heartache, rejection, self-doubt, self-loathing, and fear, there is something more to consider.

What if I told you that even when you have hit a good stride, when things are working in perfect measure, and the blueprint you've set out to draw and create is coming together better than you could have ever imagined, that even in those moments you can still be struggling?

No need to scratch your head, marinate on these words: self-indulgence, pride, conceit, and ungratefulness. Struggling at the top is just as real as struggling when you hit rock-bottom. It's something we'll explain within this journey.

My ultimate goal throughout this book is to encourage you. I will lay out some of my biggest life lessons and struggles, good and bad, in the hopes of inspiring you to build a solid foundation in faith that ignites positive actions not only in your own life but in the lives of everyone you touch. By having the proper tools, you just never know how your experiences may change someone's life. I want to feed your soul, too.

At the end of each chapter is a section called "Tools for the Toolbox." Inside you will find applicable tools for life such as words of encouragement, scripture, attributes, and practical applications that I hope will encourage your journey towards knowing or strengthening your bond with God. Life isn't easy, but if we have the tools to succeed, and grow where we know God wants us to be, our journey here on earth will always be fulfilling, no matter what may come.

You know the saying, "a carpenter is only as good as the tools in his toolbox"? The same can be said about people. We are only as good as the tools we have in our individual toolboxes of life. If we do not have the correct instruments to build upon, then it's exceptionally difficult to create a sturdy framework to live the best existence possible. Today is the day to let go of the struggle. It's time to see fully the lessons God has been whispering in your ear. It's time to live the best life you can possibly imagine! TODAY is the day! As I love saying, "Right now is the beginning of the rest of your life!" So pick up your toolbox, this carpenter wants to help you fill it up.

Chapter 2
Pouring the Footers: The Raising of a True Southern Gentleman
Luke 6:47 - 49

I remember all too clearly the day my father, Dennis, had his dreams sink before his eyes.

He had spent a great deal of time scouting the perfect property to build our family's dream home—a sizeable log cabin set on a three-acre plot amongst the towering pines and dense red cedars in the rolling hills of North Carolina. As an outdoorsman, this was my father's heaven.

The blueprints were prepared by my father's hand. As an experienced draftsman, every room was meticulously crafted in precise detail right down to the large front porch. In a fashion only my father could create, our home would be spectacular.

Having a home of your own is a big deal. It is said to be the most emotional purchase you'll ever make. It's more than a few walls to provide shelter at night; it's a soft spot to be while the outside world continues to turn. It's a place where kids should be able to play basketball in the street, ride their bikes without fear of the unknown, where sleepy-eyed homeowners should guzzle coffee and read the headlines on the front porch. It's a place where neighbors should shake hands, borrow tools, a cup of sugar, and ultimately lend a hand to anyone in the name of community.

I'm not naïve. I realize that society has lost some of these ideas, at least here in America, but that is what having a home, a solid foundation in which to grow, meant to my father. It's still the principle I hold onto when I think back to my childhood and to the things that are so different from what I witness today.

Before purchasing the land, our family lived in an apartment and a lovely home that would later become a cornerstone in my childhood. My father, being the consummate businessman he was, struck a deal with a home builder in a brand new neighborhood. The Russell family would move into the unoccupied house under a lease-to-purchase option while my father searched for the perfect parcel to clear and have a foundation poured. This was the perfect solution to a quaint place to rest our heads.

With my brother, Caleb, and me running amuck, like most parents, Dennis, and my mother, Martha, had the future of our education on their minds. I was quickly approaching my school days, and this log cabin, amongst the trees and open wilderness, would be the answer to both a home and first-rate schooling. If the build took longer than expected, the lease to purchase's school district was acclaimed as well. My father had created the best of both worlds.

Finally, the day came to clear the section of the property where our home would soon be erected. I wish I had a picture of my father's excitement that day. I was only six at the time, but having experienced plenty of exhilarating moments in my adult life I realize now that this day, this single mark on the calendar, would have been a pivotal moment in my father's existence. This was his dream. A place where he rested his hopes for his young family. That is a tremendous weight to carry as a man. A weight my father carried with remarkable strength and composure.

The grading crew arrived, ready to unsettle the rich, black earth and break ground, but something was wrong. The essential component of the plan had disappeared. The bulldozer was nowhere to be found. It had been delivered, that much everyone knew for sure, but it certainly wasn't where it had been left. It was easy to assume what had happened: the massive hunk of metal had to have been stolen.

It was a setback no one had anticipated. From the looks of things, the momentous groundbreaking would have to be put on hold until a new bulldozer could be delivered. The crew began walking the property, hopeful the machine had only been moved when they made a discovery that *literally* changed everything.

The machine had been buried. Not in the way you may be thinking; it wasn't a juvenile prank that caused a mild disruption to the day. No, it was far worse. The earth had opened under the weight of the heavy bulldozer, forcing it to tumble and be swallowed up by a sizeable sinkhole.

The foundation came out from under my father's plans that day. Our house could not be built on the property without spending thousands of dollars moving dirt and grading the land in order to protect the home from falling prey to another massive hole. It simply wasn't an option.

In one swoop, my father's dreams were shattered. The ground literally came out from under him and my mother. There would be no solid foundation to build upon, not on this property anyhow.

I can't exactly know what my father's spirit felt like that day, but I can visualize his face and imagine the internal sinking he must have felt. Life can be cruel; there is no doubt about it. To be honest, my father could have been enraged by this turn of bad luck. Even if he couldn't control every circumstance, he was a mere mortal who could have drowned himself in the loss of a dream. He could have refused to bend to the reality that what he wanted to create for his family wouldn't happen on this little piece of paradise, but that wasn't the man Dennis Russell was. He was never the one you would catch asking why, or even "why me." He simply picked himself up by his bootstraps and redirected his focus to plan B.

Reflecting back, God saved our family from further troubles that day—one of those wicked storms sailed right past us. Had the bulldozer not sank, the construction would have begun as scheduled. If the soil was that weak under the structure, our home would have been built on a ticking sinkhole. When, or if, the land gave way, the damage would have been immense. Not only that, you begin to understand that sometimes your plan B is God's plan A.

HIS plan had been working out quite well until that point. My parents were married young—high school sweethearts to be exact. My mother was fourteen when they started dating. Four years later, they said their I-do's and entered marital bliss. Neither went to college or had any formal higher education. They had love and a dream.

My father took different jobs, gaining skills as a surveyor for a water engineering company, a talented drafter, and installer of acoustical ceilings; the man was never afraid of hard work. Early in his professional career, he landed the perfect position at Clarke Industries with a little help from his brother-in-law, Joe. Dennis Russell added traveling salesman to his resume.

Clarke Industries sold high-end vacuums, pressure washers, sanders, and heavy equipment. He was a brilliant salesman. You know the old saying, "He can sell ice to Eskimos?" Well, that was him. He rose to every sales challenge given to him, but that was also just who he was in life.

That sweet eighteen-hundred-square-foot lease-to-purchase in Indian Trail, North Carolina, quickly became our solid base. Our last name would take permanent residence on the mailbox. God had already planted us right where he needed us to be. Sure, it was a complete departure from the grand log cabin in the woods. This house was tucked securely into the streets of Beacon Hills—a neighborhood where brick and siding homes with curb appeal and an occasional white picket fence sat off the road and into a scattering of towering trees. It wasn't a secluded haven by any means, but it was home.

I was not aware at the time that the life my parents created was about as beautiful as the front cover of Southern Living, as all-American as Betty Crocker, and as sweet as apple pie. All I knew was we lived like our neighbors—settled, at home, and in peace. A business deal a year before turned out to be an excellent move on my father's part. We were where we were supposed to be all along.

The Russell household was run on manners: yes sir, no sir. You called my father Mr. Russell. He had a strong distaste for when schools and the general public went away from calling adults by their surnames and casually allowed children to level the playing field and address an elder by their first name. Mr. Dennis was never an option when addressing my father. He believed that this lax view of respect was a pinprick in the dam of respect that would eventually be a push towards the decline of manners and overall respect. In calm waters even the smallest pebble can make the biggest ripples; this just so happened to be my father's pebble.

We were taught and shown love. We operated with respect and a slight fear of a wooden spoon when crossing the line. My mom worked at the fashion mart, sold Avon, and had the gift of gab. She baked. She made our school lunches every day. She decorated the house for every holiday, was a soccer mom, and just like some old black and white movie, she rang a dinner bell to call us in from playing up the street or out in the woods when something fresh was coming out of her kitchen. We went to church on

Christmas, Easter, and an occasional Sunday. We played in the great outdoors. We went camping; we hunted and learned to respect nature and how to handle a gun. We played ball in the yard. It's just the way it was.

Caleb and I shared the half-story upstairs. Across the hall, dad converted a small attic space into his workshop, reframing the walls and the floors himself. There wasn't much the man couldn't do. Not only was he a talented athlete and salesman, he was a craftsman—a true Renaissance man. He had a passion for working with his hands, and his artistry came in many forms, but the masterpieces came in the form of leather.

The way he could turn a simple dried cowhide into an exquisite self-portrait, one of Fred Bear the famous archer, will forever stand out in my memory. He made belts, belt buckles, quivers, knives, holsters, and built guns too. No matter what he was crafting, Caleb and I would sit and watch him work for hours. We spent time by his side as he imparted common sense and life lessons upon us boys. We learned the art of working until the project was complete; after all, nothing is worth doing unless it is done right. We learned patience to wait for the right thing to come and never to say the words, "I wish I had." He spoke to the importance of never making promises we could not keep, and to find your true passion in life. We also learned to foster our creative side. Dennis Russell stood for so much. I was lucky to stand by his side and learn from his well of knowledge.

I think back to what a truly incredible man he was, to the solid foundation he and my mother built for my brother and me. One moment sticks out more clearly than the others. I must have been nine or ten, which would have made Caleb seven or eight. Dad had built a treehouse out back. Caleb and I loved to run, hide amongst the falling leaves, scurry up the tree, and use our imaginations in the treehouse my father had built. I can't help but laugh at the fact that even at that age, we were tiny outdoorsmen.

We got the wild idea to rake the individual campsites off the nature trails we had created throughout the backwoods. Caleb and I would rake until there was nothing left but the exposed black earth; then we'd gather firewood and prepare campsites for our friends and neighbors to rent at their leisure. Why we ever thought our neighbors would ever come and rent a plot of circled leaves is beyond me, but my father fostered our creativity. He could have just as easily said, "Have you lost your mind? Why would anyone come and camp in our backyard?" but he didn't. Too, he could have easily told us we were wasting our time raking the backyard when we could be exerting that same energy to clean up the front, but that wasn't my father. Never once did a discouraging word slip from his mouth. Instead, he picked up a rake, scraped at the earth, and said, "Nothing is impossible."

Building great citizens, leaders, true men to go out and carve a space in this big world is a taxing job for any parent. My mother and father were exceptional. They shaped us in a way that most parents dream of doing. They

14

lived their lives under my father's words: "Nothing is impossible."

It's simple to say life was charming growing up. That isn't to say challenges didn't arise or that Caleb and I didn't dish out a fair amount of activity that was punishable, but it is to say our foundation was solid. Our parents taught us that when your personal blueprint doesn't add up, you shift your focus. As I said before, your plan B may have always been God's plan A.

Isn't that the beauty of life? If you listen and are willing to yield, God will reveal a bigger and better plan.

Tools in the Toolbox
Tool #1: Pouring the Proper Footers

Building a home has more parallels to everyday life than what may first meet the eye. Let me offer a brief overview of how a home comes to be. We first start with a blueprint—an architecturally drawn and carefully thought out plan. The design must have the ability to withstand the load-bearing weight of any and all items built on top of the foundation.

Weight is the key word here. We must consider how many rooms, bathrooms containing sinks, tubs, showers and toilets, and cabinets with shiny granite countertops will be added into the plan because with each new load added more support is needed. When the details have been settled, we must go back to the drawing board, so to speak, and make sure we have laid the proper foundation to rest all of the home's details upon. Too, each time the blueprint changes the foundation has to be made stronger.

Then comes the footers. Under every house is a foundation, under all foundations are footings. Most of the time we take the footers for granted. These wide sections poured directly into the ground and around the base of where the foundation will rest are the very thing the home will rest upon. This is where the house meets the soil, the first load-bearing structure. It's essential the footers are placed and poured correctly so that the entire home, from the rafters, support beams, and structural integrity for the rest of the house are secure and will never crack or sink.

Everything above the foundation relies upon these mighty areas of concrete. Without them, the walls will not be able to withstand the shifting of the extra weight burden onto the foundation.

These same building principals can be applied in life. If you create a plan, foresee what you plan on creating, set goals, and follow your dreams you still have to go back and make sure the proper foundation has been set to support the burdens of life, or your structure will fail. Without the proper foot placement to carry what is placed on your shoulders, you'll not be able to withstand and hold up the goals and future you are called to live.

It's so amazing to think how we start from the bottom to get to the top of anything in life, whether building a home, our spiritual faith, our career, our family, you name it, this applies. Here we conquer goals, take small steps, cash in big rewards, overcome obstacles big and small, all along making sure the foundation is unshakeable.

There is another critical element of our blueprints and foundation that I must address. As you will continue to learn and read my blueprints are uniquely mine, as yours are uniquely drawn for you. That's the beauty of blueprints; we are all created to have our own set of circumstances. Some of you may come to the table with experiences and memories of abuse, addiction, sorrow or loss. No matter what the circumstances any of us are dealt in life every "house" must be built upon the right foundation with the proper footers or the walls will come tumbling down.

Although our lives may differ from one another, we all share a common denominator in our equation of life. That is, we must be extremely careful in pouring the foundation upon which we stand. Reevaluate your blueprints, your goals and dreams. Think about your foundation. Where does it lie? Look around; are the walls of your life crumbling down? Are there areas requiring extra support in order to recalculate the load and weight you are adding on top? If necessary, add a few more footers and alter the burden of the extra weight.

Don't look for peers to prop up the sides; it's time to refocus the blueprint. It's time to dig deep, change your foundation, and create a life with purpose.

The best scripture addressing this very issue is *Luke 6:47- 49.* It reads

> [47] As for everyone who comes to me and hears my words and puts them into practice, I will show you what they are like. [48] They are like a man building a house, who dug down deep and laid the foundation on rock. When a flood came, the torrent struck that house but could not shake it, because it was well built. [49] But the one who hears my words and does not put them into practice is like a man who built a house on the ground without a foundation. The moment the torrent struck that house, it collapsed, and its destruction was complete.

Don't let the torrent strike and create destruction. Change the base. It's amazing what a little reengineering will do for your life. If you can make these changes, or already know your foundation is sound, tool #1, pouring the footers, is ready to be used to its fullest. Toss it in your toolbox and come along.

Chapter 3
Hitting the Nail on the Head

God's plan for me was evolving and shined early on. I was born on Halloween. In fact, when I was a child I thought everyone dressed up and handed out candy because it was my birthday. It was an honest mistake. It's what every kid would feel if their special day ended with elaborate costumes and enough candy to fill a convenience store instead of a simple cake and some half-deflated balloons. It seemed logical enough actually. My mother reassured me that wasn't the case, but I'm sure if you asked her today she still gets a kick out of that notion.

A birthday on Halloween produced an extra layer of excitement and added to the joy of my celebration; it also meant I had to sit on the sidelines and wait for a full school year to pass before I was allowed to enter Kindergarten. My birthday fell a few days after the registration cutoff. While the other five-year-olds were at school, I was building forts and building tree houses to play war with Caleb. We lived in the great outdoors, riding our bikes everywhere so we might stumble across a hidden treasure of the neighborhood. I used my imagination and created my own crazy sense of reality.

That year passed, summer faded away. By the time next year rolled around, I entered Kindergarten and within two months I was a year older than my entire class. For some, being the oldest would be a problem—an extra sense of dutiful responsibility that the majority doesn't want to have fall on their shoulders. For me, it was a blessing. I was taller, stronger, more mature, and it gave me a different type of perspective. That may sound off for a six-year-old, but a year, especially at that age, creates a noticeable difference.

I enjoyed searching for the perfect shade of green to color the maple or pine tree and made certain I tinted the sun with hues of golden yellow and bright bursts of orange while the majority of the other kids scribbled in a rainbow of unlikely color combinations. I was also different than the others because I was left-handed. While the school and my teachers may have seen it as a burden, attempting to convert me to a right-hander was not an option. Both my mom and dad were left-handed, and that is how I learned, it's what I knew. They taught me from an early age that people who are left-handed are said to use the right side of their brain more, which is considered to be the creative side. I saw this as an advantage and started to understand where my need to stay within the lines and pick the perfect shade of color was coming from. In the end, I would have to overcome the challenges of a dominant right-handed world. Even then, I loved a good challenge.

One of my all-time favorite shirts read, "Everyone is born right-handed, but only the greatest can overcome it." I wish I still had it now. It made me proud of this difference, even if it isn't such a big issue in schools now. It was then. I was okay with searching for the only pair of green-handled scissors at the bottom of the bucket of fifty others.

I truly believe I was born with an affinity for crafting the finest details in everything I do, just as my father had done before me. Combine that with an eye for precision, even at that early age, and the ability to think both in and outside the box, and adults began to take notice. Still, I cannot say that there was a lesson on the blackboard that resonated with me and created the person I was then or even now.

When words like "leadership potential," "example," and "rule follower" get tossed in your direction, that immediately sets you ahead of the class and cultivates a breeding ground for success.

Even with all those factors, I still felt like I kept missing the head of the nail. I was different. Not in a negative way. I was considered to be of the popular crowd and had many friends. I was just different than the rest of my peers. Internally, I questioned why I made the choices I did. I wondered why I had this bubbling sense of responsibility inside me when it hadn't yet developed in others. Why I took it upon myself to do the right thing at every turn. That mischievous little devil that sits on everyone's shoulder didn't have a strong enough whisper to cause me to falter from a straight and narrow path. I suppose that is what people mean by saying someone is an "old soul." Those feelings continued until I found my way to middle school. It was there that my path opened up, and the beginning stages of my life's purpose began to reveal themselves.

As kids do, I joined as many clubs and sports as I found interesting. I was lean and muscular, which made me quick on the track, basketball court, and football fields. Between clubs and athletics, I began testing my true leadership skills. If there was a role to step into, mainly the president's seat, I took it. Don't get me wrong, it wasn't for bragging rights. I enjoyed these roles—it was a natural fit. Still, taking on the president of student body or yearbook or your sports team, does tend to separate you from your peers. It garners the right kind of attention. That was evident in the seventh grade.

Districts across North Carolina submitted a handful of seventh and eighth-grade students to attend an innovative program called the Legislator School for Youth Leadership Development or LSYLD. The conference was held at Western Carolina University. Each school was allowed to select only one boy and one girl from its entire student body to enter into the selection process. I caught word my name had been tossed into the mix and later I was selected. It was an honor, yet, at the time, I had no idea the magnitude of what I was in for. Nor did I realize that this extraordinary opportunity would change my scope from an inward approach to leadership to something more far-reaching. A few months later, I packed my bags, gave up an entire month of my summer break, and headed for the mountains.

Upon arriving it was clear, this "school" was different. This wasn't your typical sleepaway summer camp. There would be no childish games, campfires, and sing-alongs on the month-long docket. Of course, it wasn't all business, there were plenty of opportunities to play. We got to select exciting team building adventures like white water rafting. While these adventures were exhilarating, they also proved to be lessons in leadership and teamwork. We were taught that with good time management and hard work you are allowed to play as well. These lessons were carried throughout the camp.

As I stepped out of the car, I realized I was among the best of the best. The air was buzzing with the qualities I most admired. It was evident in the way everyone carried themselves. I remember thinking I was about to embark on the experience of a lifetime.

Ultimately, the goal of the conference was to create better communicators, teach and foster conflict resolution skills, problem-solving strategies, core values, time management, and the list goes on. LSYLD wasn't simply there to create future leaders; its goal was to churn out senators, political powerhouses, community leaders, and entrepreneurs. In short, we were walking in as kids and were expected to leave with the fundamentals of excellent adults. These four weeks further laid the framework for my solid foundation.

With that, I suppose it should go without saying, the experience was one for the record books and it left a lifetime mark on me. For the first time in life, my place on this earth was clearly defined. Here I was away from home with the greatest youth leaders from around my state, and I belonged. I felt normal—accepted. I was completely at home. I was surrounded by people who didn't get in trouble, had like minds, were comfortable with who they were, and took life seriously. All of these things were things I had struggled with before I arrived. Seeing these characteristics in others allowed me to relax and be who God had destined me to be with no apologies or awkward feeling of trying to be different.

At the end of the conference, awards were handed out. All of the characteristics I learned about myself were highlighted on a manila 8x11 framed certificate with my name in big, bold letters. It read: Legislators' School for Youth Development at Western Carolina University awards A Peer Helper Scholarship to Brandon Russell. This meant I had secured a spot to return the following year and act as a counselor to a new class of leaders. Who I was then and who I continue to strive to be today was summed up in a few simple words—Peer Helper. It was the highlight of my middle school career.

When I settled back at home, I had to readjust my thinking. I was moping. I didn't jump back into riding bikes with my friends. I hung around the house and didn't engage. I longed to be back amongst such great leaders. I knew I would have another opportunity to return, but it felt like an impossibly long wait. The knowledge and acceptance of myself were immense up in those mountains. I had to flip the switch, so to speak, solidly plant my feet on that growing foundation and incorporate those feelings into my life at home, not just while I was away.

My mother came to me and laid out the facts: There isn't a perfect world, especially not at that age. I had to continue on and be a kid. If I didn't straighten up and snap out of my funk, I wasn't going to be allowed to attend the next session. That did the trick, let me tell you. Life marched on.

The school year came and went. I did participate in the next leadership session. Again, it was life-changing. Those days are still some of the largest stepping stones my path has seen up until now.

God was moving in my life at this tender age, even if I didn't know *Him* the way I do now. Yet, it wasn't until high school that I came to understand there was something deeper missing in my life.

The same sense of responsibility I felt in my early childhood days extended into my teens. I attended a small 2A school where all roughly eight hundred students knew each other or, at least, knew about one another.

I didn't fall into the traps life sets before most teenagers. I chose a life free of teenage drinking, smoking, and life-altering choices. I held myself to a higher standard, knowing that one day those decisions could, and most likely would, come back to stir up trouble in the life I was creating for myself. My head was firmly on my shoulders, and my eyes were always set towards the future. I worked with the D.A.R.E. (Drug Abuse Resistance Education) program and taught the effects of drugs and alcohol to younger grades. I learned so much working with this program that I made the choice not to drink until I was twenty-two. While I took a visible and audible stance, I never passed judgment on those who didn't subscribe to my same line of thinking. That isn't in my nature.

Of course, I found myself in places where these types of activities were taking place—whether a Friday night high school party or later in college—but, it just wasn't for me. When I was asked why I didn't drink or do drugs, I used to tell everyone that it was because I was high on life. I didn't need anything extra; my crazy energy was enough to have fun at any time. The other factor was my reach from serving as the student body president, which thrusted me in the forefront of my class. I realized then that my life had to be a walking example.

A friend named Ellis Austin would often mention the fun activities he had in store over the weekend. The majority of them surrounded his youth group. The idea intrigued me. I wasn't a foreigner to ways of organized religion. I had spent plenty of my younger days among the worshippers at our local church, but up until this point, the vast majority of my weekends had been spent at Lake Norman on Outrigger Harbor.

My parents had purchased an RV; a nice one that had all the comforts of home. On a rentable plot of land, close to the rippling waters of Lake Norman, my father spent hours creating a screened porch and an outdoor kitchenette with a full-sized refrigerator and plenty of counter space. This was a home away from home for us, but it also meant our fellowship was done with friends and not inside a chapel.

Not to say those times weren't extraordinary because they were immensely special. Our little community consisted of four families, including my own. The dads hit the water in their Hobie cat regattas or behind a boat on their skis. I can still see the mixture of crisp white sails weaving between sails of bright colors, each flapping in the breeze while zipping across the deep blue waters of the lake. The beauty was second to none.

Weekend after weekend, four families came together on the docks with the sun beating against our skin and the deep red clay sinking between our toes. For roughly eight years, this was our life. It came to a halt when the owner of the harbor sold the land to a huge developer. A country club for the elite was erected and we lost our option to lease the land. Our little slice of paradise was cleared to make way for roughly ten stately homes. Such is life, I guess you would say.

With the constant schedule of being home on the weekends, I decided Ellis's youth group sounded intriguing. During my first visit, I came to realize many of my friends were members too. It drew me in. After a few visits, Caleb decided to join me.

The church had a new young pastor named Jim. He took an instant liking to me and I to him. He quickly became a force in my life, encouraging me to find my place with God, to live and be the shining light of what a Christ-centered life looked and felt like—which truthfully, I had been living but was missing the weekly dose of His word, which feeds the soul. My guest seat among the youth group quickly became a saved seat with my name on it.

The youth went on a ski trip during winter break. Caleb and I hit the slopes too. During that time I knew the gentle knock God had placed on my heart for a number of years could only be answered inside the church. My heart was on fire for God, but still I had questions.

Every Sunday for the next seven months, I was in the pews with a hymnal in hand and a song in my heart. Within the first month and a half of attending, my mom began to stand next to Caleb and me with the same fire bubbling in her soul. My father was missing, though. He wasn't a man who often found his way into the house of God. He attended when one of us boys was involved in something special, like the Christmas pageant, but for the most part, Dennis Russell wasn't one who would be standing among the worshippers.

That was okay. His haven was the outdoors. I never questioned him. After spending all week working, and often traveling away from home, my dad preferred spending time on island hunts, practicing at the Indian Trail Bow Club, at the gun range sharpening his skills, or simply cutting the grass to keep up with his award-winning curb appeal. It's what the man loved. At the time, it didn't bother me that my father's relationship with God was different than my own. You pick your battles, as they say, and this particular issue wasn't a place I rested my battle cry. That would come much later. His weekends were his weekends, at least that is what he used to say.

For those seven months, I listened. I asked questions. I grew a bountiful faith and passion for Christ. I took roles within the youth group. The younger students were drawn to me, and I was helping them grow while I grew. Still, there was something more I needed to know. When would my time come? How would I know that I was fully ready to hand my heart over to Jesus? The answer was eluding me.

Any given Sunday, I listened to Pastor Jim ask the congregation to bow our heads in prayer. During that time, he called us. As ministers do, he asked for anyone wanting to turn their life over to God and be saved to simply walk down the long aisles to the front of the pulpit to those waiting with open arms. With eyes half-opened, I watched others take that march towards salvation. I kept digging into my own heart looking for that place within me to be awakened and lead me without question down the passageway to full forgiveness. When that awakening didn't come, I asked a friend how I would know when it was my time. All she could say was, "You'll know it when you feel it." I couldn't understand what she meant by feel it.

Each Sunday I asked myself the same question, "Do you feel it yet?"

The answer was always no. I felt nothing different. I was filled with Christ, but something hadn't fully taken hold.

"When?" I prayed, "When?"

After a sizeable amount of soul-searching and prayer, one beautiful Sunday morning, I stood in the pews. My hands were folded as I prayed silently to myself. The time of the service where Pastor Jim called us to follow our heart was coming. Something changed in those moments.

The hymn *Jesus Is Tenderly Calling* was echoing through the chapel and pulling at my heart. As the music rose and touched the rafters, I started sweating. God was there. In all those moments of questioning, wondering, digging into my soul, and countless prayers I had no idea the door to my heart wasn't fully open. But at that moment, it was.

Everything inside me felt like it was instantly exposed. If I hadn't known better, I could have sworn someone behind me poured a pot of boiling hot water over my head. Scorching heat singed down from the top of my head and rushed to the toes in my shoes.

My sins were boiled to the surface and rinsed away. The bacteria of life was gone; I felt new and clean. I was now whole and filled with determined purpose.

In those moments, while Jesus was tenderly calling, I let Him in.

I looked over at my friend, the one I had questioned so many times when I would know if I were ready to accept God. With tears streaming down my face, I said, "It's happening. I can feel it. It's happening."

The tears pouring from my eyes were suddenly matched by her own. God had saved me. I slipped from my place in the pew, and I let the tears of joy filling my heart carry me down the aisle to where Pastor Jim stood. This was my moment.

A light and fire ignited in those moments. Faith had found me in a new way—a faith that was strong and everlasting. Pastor Jim's arms were waiting; they opened and then closed around me as we prayed together. In those moments, Jim pronounced his excitement for this life-turning event. It was one he had been praying about for many months. God shined his miraculous light that day. I just happened to be the one who received the gift—what a beautiful gift it was and still is.

Baptisms came shortly after. A deeper understanding of God's path was once again laid out. I picked up the torch and carried it forward. Others came to know God when I was asked to knock on their hearts. When we are called, all we have to do is answer. These days became the real definition of Colossians 3:12.

The Tools in the Toolbox
Tool #2: Acceptance

"God has chosen you. You are holy and loved by Him. Because of this, your new life should be full of loving-pity. You should be kind to others and have no pride. Be gentle and be willing to wait for others." Colossian 3:12

In this chapter, we have addressed acceptance. Acceptance, according to the definition, is the act of taking or receiving something offered. A favorable reception; approval; favor; and lastly, being accepted or acceptable.

In today's society of social media and oversaturation of available media, many people struggle with feeling accepted. There are two important points of acceptance which I want to point out. Both are powerful tools that you can carry throughout your walk and journey in life.

Within one scenario I explained how I had a textbook normal childhood. I did the things most kids and young men do while growing up, yet there was something inside me that some do not experience.

I enjoyed being a leader—that isn't for everyone. I welcomed challenges—some feel challenges put too much emotional strain on their hearts, minds, and spirit. I love being a problem solver—for some that is stressful. Regardless of where you stand on these matters, we still seek acceptance within ourselves and others in order to find the places we feel most comfortable.

It wasn't until I attended the leadership conference that it all clicked. I was wrestling with insecurity. I wondered if people thought I was a so-called "brown-noser" and a "goodie-goodie" that never did anything wrong. I did do things wrong, trust me. While being a good kid isn't a true "issue" it does make you feel different than the kid cashing in on negative attention.

At the conference, I was amongst my peers. These were kids just like me. I finally realized that I had found my place. Sometimes that takes time, sometimes it happens naturally, but either way, there are groups and places in this big world for every single person. I realized too that like every major corporation there is still only one Chief Executive Officer among the thousands of employees. I wanted to live my life like the "CEOs" of the world. I wanted to set examples and lead. It just clicked. This was my place.

Each of us is cut from a different cloth, so to speak, and honestly, there is nothing wrong with that. Some want to be the President, some want to be firefighters, some want to be stay-at-home parents; whatever you choose, be what you were created to be! I do not have a musical bone in my body, but I wish I did. I cannot make my living rushing the football up the field for the game-winning touchdown, but I think it would be fun. I choose to make the gifts and talents unique to me and use them as I was created in God's perfection. I encourage you to do the same. What's your best gift? Do you accept that talent? Do you accept you are here to give that gift to others?

ACCEPT who you are! God makes no mistakes!

That is the other part of acceptance we touched upon—acceptance of God coming into my heart. Although I may have always believed in a higher power, I had never truly accepted and allowed him into my heart. There is a significant difference between believing and accepting.

God's gift of forgiveness is free. It comes without any strings attached. So often people believe you must live a perfect life to accept God. That isn't the definition of faith or acceptance. Plus, we are fallible humans. Perfection simply isn't possible! Accepting God and asking for his forgiveness is actually acknowledging to him that you are not perfect, and you will make mistakes. This is as much personal acceptance as it is Godly acceptance.

Early in my life, I did not equate my actions with my spiritual side; I was just someone who understood respect. It took until I was seventeen to accept God. That acceptance comes at different times for everyone. Some are born knowing and accepting; some come into acceptance at seventeen or fifty or eighty-eight. Whatever the age or time, God is always waiting for acceptance from you. If you can accept your place in life, all the reasons why you are here to share your own unique talents, you have tool #2, acceptance, ready to use to its fullest. Toss it in your toolbox and come along.

Chapter 4
Planting the Mustard Seed
"Great things grow from small beginnings."
Proper 6:11

I had accepted God which ignited faith in my new beginning. I knew that faith would grow into something immense. At the time I took the walk down the aisle to accept the Lord, I had no idea what my faith would look like. I only knew I was clean, free, and starting over, reborn as a Christian.

In the book of Mark 4:30 – 32 the parable of the Mustard Seed is told. If you are not familiar with the story, I'll give you the abridged version.

A mustard seed is tiny—comparable to the size of a peppercorn, yet it's smaller.

It's so small, in fact, if you held the little brownish-yellow seed in your palm and accidently dropped it on the ground, it's highly unlikely you would ever find it again.

Even though the mustard seed is tiny, it's mighty. So hardy that when planted it grows so large that birds can perch on its branches. It's even strong enough to hold their nest. Some grow into trees that stand twenty feet tall. It's miraculous how something so small can grow into something that cannot be swayed by the wind.

That is why Jesus likened the Kingdom of Heaven to this tiny wonder. When He began his earthly ministry, he had no followers. The Bible tells of when Jesus began walking along the shores of Galilee when he saw Peter and his brother Andrew.

"Come, follow me," Jesus said.

Peter and Andrew did as they were commanded to do, and continued to follow until Jesus gathered the twelve disciples. It was a small, honest beginning, much like the mustard seed. Jesus planted those twelve disciples to spread his word, and it would help the Kingdom of God to grow. As the seed of faith was planted, the Kingdom grew and grew until it became the seed of faith that no wind could sway.

After accepting God, I began planting my own small seeds.

In the months leading up to my graduation from high school, the next step in my formal education was on my mind. With a fist full of options, my decision of which University I would attend was not taken lightly; in fact, it was a very calculated one. I had three schools of interest. The first was the University of North Carolina. It was a natural choice as I have Carolina "blue blood" running through my veins, as I have religiously pulled for the Carolina Tar Heels basketball team since I played in middle school.

I should also mention that when it comes to college football, I bleed SEC, Georgia Bulldog red specifically, but the University of Georgia wasn't within my realm of consideration. My parents were paying for my education, and I wanted to stay respectfully within North Carolina and take advantage of in-state tuition. It was the least I could do when they were bestowing this blessing upon me.

The next option was to hit the coast. The University of Wilmington would offer a solid education conveniently located by the waves and the coastal water I so greatly love. But when it came down to it, the most important factor was who had the finest business school in the entire state of North Carolina. In order to be the successful entrepreneur I was striving to be, I knew I needed to learn from the very best.

That opened my eyes to Appalachian State University, nestled in the mountains of Boone, North Carolina. Its ranking as the top business school in the Southeast made it a no-brainer to add to my list of choices.

The letters came and one by one I had been accepted into my top choices. This was a dream, but narrowing down which university I would call home was a tough process. I had always visualized myself as a Tar Heel, but I had to make a smart business decision. The University of North Carolina was three times the size of the other two universities I had set my sights on. Being one in a class of four hundred didn't settle well. I wanted to be in a more intimate classroom environment. Somewhere I felt I was given more of an opportunity to be hands on and learn. I knew what I had to do, and I let go of the idea of UNC.

The University of North Carolina Wilmington had just received their accreditation in business the year prior and was new to the business scene. Two attempts to obtain more information about their program fell on deaf ears and thus I finally made the decision to attend Appalachian State University.

Despite the difficult decision of narrowing down what would be best in the long run, I had no idea what God was building in my path. As my father had experienced, I know now that His plan A was definitely in the works. My foundation and framework would be vastly grown upon my arrival. It's also true that had I gone to either of the other choices the likelihood of being the Brandon Russell you know now wouldn't have happened. I would most likely be known only as Brandon Russell, CEO, than Brandon Russell celebrity carpenter.

Before I packed my bags, my father came to me. I specifically remember him sitting me down and saying he wanted me to join a fraternity. Shocked and questioning his motives, at first, he had peaked my curiosity enough to ask him why and how he had come to this decision.

Neither he nor my mom had attended college, and honestly, I couldn't fathom what would drive his line of thinking. The same standards I prided myself on weren't exactly in line with the general "norms" of what I envisioned fraternity life to be. Then I asked him why his reasoning was sound. At this time, statistically speaking, out of all the Fortune 500 companies' Chief Executive Officers, eighty percent belonged to a Greek organization. With wisdom prevailing, my father said that this society of men would help me develop character, strengthen my respect for tradition, and develop an uncommon bond of brotherhood between men.

It would teach me leadership in a different capacity. If I had the ability to lead a group of headstrong men, all coming to the table from countless backgrounds, all living and operating under different perspectives and motives, I would develop the necessary skills to lead any boardroom. This experience would be a good lesson in people if nothing else. It also had the potential to teach me rejection. That mighty nine-letter word wasn't something I was too familiar with at the time. Bottom line, I would be judged. I would be scrutinized in a way I had not been before. Would I be "good enough" to be among this brotherhood of men? Deep down I knew real leaders are the ones who are willing to be judged, disapproved of, and not flinch if they are not always among the popular vote.

There was something else churning up concern inside me too. I didn't drink. Naturally, I was worried that there was no way a fraternity would ever think I was cool or acceptable if I didn't partake like everyone else. With my stubborn pride, I knew I was not going to push my morals aside, and I was scared of not getting a bid because I refused to drink.

I suppose you are wondering why drinking was such an issue for me. It comes down to a simple fact. I know myself better than anyone else. I know what pulls at my insides. To be blunt, I have a very addictive personality. I didn't need alcohol, but I was afraid it may need me if the taste passed my lips. If I like something, no one will be able to stop me from doing it.

Thankfully, I have an even stronger drive to overcome that piece of me. It's the same drive I told you I was born with, and I knew to accomplish what I set forth to do I would have to stand firm and not allow anything to get in my way. My foundation was strong, and I knew if rejection came because I refused to relax my beliefs, then it was rejection I was happy to take.

With my father's unwavering logic by my side, when Rush week came, I put myself out there. With eleven fraternities on campus, it was impossible to rush every organization so I did as I always do, I did my research. I narrowed my options based on what each chapter stood for, their beliefs, characteristics, and history of how and when they were formed. This was more to me than just an extracurricular activity to say I was a part of; this would be a newfound brotherhood that was a forever commitment.

In all, I rushed four fraternities, and four bids came. While it was flattering, there was only one that stood out soundly above the rest—Delta Chi, a group of men, of bonded brothers, who were about more than just a good time. These were driven, focused leaders that had learned to balance having a good time with developing a sound education, while holding prominent leadership roles on campus. My concern was put to ease. I knew they would respect my decisions and not judge me for not drinking or using drugs of any sort. The chapter's motto was my life motto. Needless to say, I wanted in.

Thus began my journey as a Delta Chi. The other fraternities had houses on campus—we did too—but there was one other advantage we had over every other fraternity. We also had a fraternity hall in the dorms. It wasn't just any dorm, though. It just so happened to be on the fourth floor of Cone Hall. We were conveniently located in the middle of three sororities above us and three below us. Trust me, no one was complaining. It was a small slice of heaven to be honest. I immediately stepped up and took on the role of Pledge Class President.

This role suited me well, and my seed of leadership was planted within the fraternity. I wasn't there just for fun and games. Everything I did I came to with a business sense. In short, I wanted to keep the fraternity on the rise.

There was something else that came to my attention in those days. Fraternity member composites, the once-a-year framed collage of pictures featuring the brothers that came before me, were lined perfectly down the hallway. Beyond the names and perfectly coiffed hair, something struck me as odd. Prior to 1990, the composites had a title that was now missing from every composite taken from 1990 to 1994. During the four years before my arrival, the title of Chaplain was nowhere to be found under anyone's name. It was then that the mustard seed was planted.

Let's face it, things could have gone differently. I had a newfound freedom. I was away from home. I had the ability to make my own "rules" and decisions. My parents were not there to govern my every move as they had been for the eighteen years prior. My chance to make something of myself while standing on my own two feet had arrived. I had two options the day I noticed my brothers were without a leader in Christ. One, I could ignore this fact, carry on in my own faith without sharing it with others, or I could take God's nudge.

My mustard seed was watered that day. I felt compelled to lead. If there was one thing I knew how to do, it was this. After gaining permission to take over the abandoned position, my first mission was to lead a group Bible study. I took the role seriously. God had a place in my fraternity as much as he had a place inside me.

I worked, organized, and put a call out to hear God's message. If I recall correctly, roughly thirteen eager brothers showed up to share in God's word. I knew in my heart of hearts that I could do more. Being that we were in the middle of six sorority halls, I approached each of them individually to see what their interest would be in hosting a joint Bible study. With a resounding yes, brothers and sisters were united. During the next meeting with my brothers, I slid in the fact the Chi Omega sorority would be joining us that week, and needless to say there were more than double the brothers at the next Bible study. Whether their real intentions were to hear God's word or simply give a good showing for the girls, it didn't matter because what happened was incredible.

My brothers and myself for that matter were given a gift. We all realized that we would be hearing different perspectives and views of the opposite sex relating to God, the Bible, life issues, faith, and living as a Christian while under the heated temptations of college. The experience was eye-opening and enlightening.

We continued the Bible studies, and new brothers stepped up to lead as Chaplain. God's love and grace overpowered ill intention and sinful temptation through the powerful message of ministry. It was rewarding to see the mustard seed bloom and take shape. Four brothers came to know and accept Christ in those days. It all started with a simple request to be the church amongst the fraternity. I hold these days very dear and close to my heart. I was called. This was the example God wanted me to live.

Those days set me up for the next natural leadership role. I decided to take on the task of Community Service Chair—which I gladly took on with one goal in mind: I was on a mission to change the stereotype and remove the stigma surrounding Greek life as a whole. Admittedly, even I had that same label in my mind before attending college. I wanted to prove to the community that we cared, had compassion, were there to serve them, and that we were not there to cause disruption and party.

I knew where I could make the biggest impact—the wide creek bordering the university's intramural athletic fields. It had sadly become a dumping ground for used tires and endless amounts of debris. It was an eyesore, to say the least, and one I knew we had the ability to fix.

I once again turned to the sororities, this time, in particular, the ladies of Kappa Delta. The call went out. The troops were rallied, and approximately ninety people showed up to roll up their sleeves and make an outstanding difference.

We worked for hours. By the time we had collected everything within our reach, the place looked like a landfill. The trash was piled well over our heads. I had coordinated with the local waste management services to haul the trash away. As they arrived, so too did the newspaper. We all lined up, symbolizing that fraternities and sororities were united to make a difference. Sure, we reeked of trash, were covered in dirt and grime, but the only thing anyone smelled was the scent of victory and accomplishment. Our photos were snapped.

Later the headline read something to the effect of "Don't Trash Fraternities and Sororities." I cannot recall the exact wording all these years later, but what I do recall is seeing the hard work and dedication to a simple plan come to fruition. Like the seed coming into its fruit-bearing season, this was ours.

We were called to do good, to make an impact on others in a way that would benefit the community. One small seed, one big reaction.

Soon after the trash collection occurred came one of the most critical roles of the chapter—Rush Chair for the fall class of 1995. While this may not seem like a big deal, it was. I hadn't been a brother for a full year yet. The only rush I had experienced was my own. How would I be able to pull off taking over this task?

The details of how seemed insignificant, more important was my willingness to figure it out. The challenge was set and as always, I took this next step up the ladder to heart, by rising to the occasion.

Rush arrived, and with it came the largest rush attendance up until that date. With all of this under my belt, a record-breaking rush and pledge class, I was ready to serve on the executive board. The nominations were placed. My eyes were set on the Vice President's chair. Mind you, I still hadn't technically been a brother for a full year yet, but that fact was once again overlooked.

It was a close race, but I won the seat of Vice President. I served diligently during the spring semester until the acting President had to step down due to a personal matter. I was inducted and sworn in as the new President. With excitement and extreme pressure, I took the reins. Here I was, the youngest President, nurturing and guiding ninety-six brothers, within the largest fraternity on campus, as a sophomore. You read that right, as a sophomore. The pressure of having older members looking to me to lead them was nerve-racking to say the least, but deep down I knew this is where I would thrive.

That isn't to say my father wasn't right. This was a group of determined men. For some, this was their first taste of freedom. They chose to do as they pleased. It's said, "conflict and chaos build character." Those days prepared me to be able to tackle any role of leadership I took from then after. My dad hit the nail on the head with this one. I wouldn't take back a single cherished moment from my days in the fraternity. Delta Chi truly helped mold the man I am today.

God's seed was growing.

Tools in the Toolbox
Tool #3: Caring for the Seed

In this chapter, I speak of planting the mustard seed—the tiny seed that can grow into something so mighty.

So often in life, we plant a seed but never take the time to nourish it with the proper nutrients and fertilizer. Without care, a small seed cannot grow to reach its fullest potential. If we simply expect a plant to use only the nutrients that are already in the soil, so to speak, we are not giving the seed a fair shot at blossoming.

This goes hand in hand with life. When you find a passion for something you love, for instance, mine is leadership, you must feed the need. I fed the leadership seed by taking positions that helped me grow in all facets of life. If I allowed possible rejection to reign over my decisions, especially during my college career, I would have never grown and firmly developed the roots I gained. I can now firmly say the roots of my leadership seed are able to withstand the turbulent winds of both rejection and losses. But that is only because I still continue to feed the need of the seed I planted so long ago. Just like a plant in your garden, after it blooms, you still need to give it food and water to allow it to thrive.

What seeds have you planted? Do you water them or do you leave it to chance and let the potential plant wither away before it has peeked through the soil? It's imperative to water and feed your desires, as long as they are healthy and move you forward in life and in faith.

47

There is another key element to feeding the need. Our inward approach to growing must also be an outward approach for sharing the spoils of the seed. We plant the seed because we have a desire to create a mighty crop, but the beauty we are creating inward can be used to feed others too. It's two-fold.

If we complement and encourage others in their needs and choices in life, we fertilize their soil and help them continue to grow and flourish in their gifts and talents. If we all take this approach, imagine how big the garden of life can grow!

If I were not accepted and had been rejected for my choice not to drink or participate in things that did not feed my soul, I would never have become who I am today. The fraternity was my nutrient, the soil that fed the seedling and allowed my personal garden to shape others.

So here is the challenge I propose to you: think of one area in your life that needs fertilizing. Does it need more soil to keep the roots strong? How about water? Does it need to be dug up and a new seed planted in its place? What moves you forward?

Take time to water your seeds, you'll never know how mighty the plant is if you never take the time to do the most basic gardening. As you are now seeing, sometimes we need more than one tool to tweak the most basic foundation. There is plenty of room for more tools in the toolbox. You now have tool #3, caring for the seed, to use to its fullest. Toss it in your toolbox and come along.

Chapter 5
My Greatest Sin
"If you think you are not conceited, it means you are very conceited indeed."
C. S. Lewis, *Mere Christianity*

Sir Isaac Newton said it best: "For every action, there is an equal and opposite reaction."

I wouldn't be much of a man or a Christian if I didn't share my *whole* truth. I have shortcomings and a bag of misgivings. Even putting those words in ink is difficult. When we are forced to look inward and pull out all the questionable pieces of ourselves, it tends to upset the soul. This is a part of my journey that I promised, in the beginning, I would hand over to you. While I have now rectified these moments that do not do justice to the man I am now, please remember, we are all merely human. We struggle. We make mistakes.

During those days as Delta Chi's President, I had begun making a name for myself on campus. My leadership roles within the fraternity quickly lent itself to making waves campus-wide.

The university's eyes were upon me. I received the Senator of the Year Award, an award given by the Student Government Association. I found my way into the CSIL, Center for Student Involvement and Leadership Office. I was soon approached to be the first President of a newly founded club called Club Council. The council was tasked with governing all of the organizations and clubs at

Appalachian State. This in and of itself was a monumental task. From there came an invitation to sit on the Chancellors' Board. My role was to be the student voice when it came to student affairs.

My plate was full to say the least. Understand—I'm not giving you my list of accolades to impress—I'm actually building up the platform from which I was soon to teeter off.

My greatest sin, which was that of pride, was planted and became a monster I continued to feed. Pride does something to a person. When used wrong, it takes control. It makes you behave in a manner that hurts others, and places blame in other people's court. It's a nasty sin that can destroy everything good you've done if you let it. This simple concept took a long time to understand. With pride as the seed, my fertilizer was laced with conceit.

The attention I was getting, the fact that the faculty knew my name, the sororities, the fraternities, the organizations, and the students, began to make my head swell. The attention on my achievements was one thing, but the attention I was receiving over my looks was a whole other monster. I started training harder in the gym. My body responded quickly. All of this became a recipe for disaster. My ego went into overload.

My blinders were on, and I kept looking forward, not considering the damage being done, and simply never looking back. I was on a mission. I was building the Brandon Russell Empire.

I was so foolish. What I did not understand was if I had taken the time to look back, I would have known what was being said, how I was making others feel, and what my so-called empire really looked like in the eyes of others. My ego and obsession to be on top and be the absolute very best had grabbed the best parts of me—the gentle parts that really only wanted the best for everyone.

 I wasn't the nicest. That isn't a statement that is easy to say and one that I frankly find embarrassing. I did whatever it took to accomplish what I felt was right because again I was Brandon Russell. I had built myself up to live under the pretense that whatever I said was the way it should be. If I said it, then it must be right.

Worse, my ego not only grew from power and respect, but it grew with physical dominance too. The eyes of the world were on me, the same way the eyes in the mirror reflected back to me, and shamefully, I loved it.

Soon I expected to walk into a room and be noticed. I heard what the girls were saying when I passed by. I knew what they wanted, and I was not afraid to show it. I was spinning out of control. My values, my convictions, my hard-earned name were becoming a joke. This sinful seed was massive by now. The new branches of pride and conceit were starting to suck the life out of everything.

I wish I could say something happened and I snapped out of it soon after the plant began to grow, but that isn't the truth. I purposefully started to use my power and prowess within the fraternity on the brothers I so greatly loved. I did whatever it took to get my way. However, I must make it clear that not everything I did was done with malice because it wasn't. I still did amazing things to further my leadership along. I have a huge heart and luckily God's love is always stronger than Satan's sinful temptation. Pieces of me still shined through, but I was walking a very thin line.

The greatest example of my greatest sin came my junior year if memory serves me correctly. The brothers gathered in the lobby of the fraternity hall for a game of Charades. The pledges were the actors, and no brother was safe from scrutiny. If you have never played Charades, the game's objective is to act out a scene, person, or place and have the audience guess what you are acting out. Generally, you are not allowed to talk, but for this game, it was allowed. Obviously, the actors were not allowed to give a name or certain obvious facts, but still speaking was allowed.

Up pops a pledge with one specific member in mind. He made his way in front of the mirror beside the elevator doors and began looking at himself. The acts that followed reddened my face. His hands flew to his hair, rubbing them vigorously through; he kissed his bicep while winking at himself. His words became daggers.

"I look better than everybody. I am in perfect shape. Look at my biceps. No one is better than me. Man, I look good."

My heart was pounding. I remember thinking to myself he better not be doing an impression of me. I knew the truth, though. So did everyone else. One of the brothers loudly said, "That's easy, Brandon Russell."

The pledge laughed. So did everyone else when he replied, "Yep." I laughed too, but only on the outside. My insides were fuming. Internally, my mind raced. What are they laughing at, I thought. I do so much for this fraternity! I bust my tail to give them everything they want and have. I do all of this! It is me, not them!

Instead of hearing their words, understanding this was the outside view of the man that stared back at me in the mirror, I let my ego ramp up to full force. I chalked up his words and their laughter to nothing but pitiful jealousy. They were all naysayers. They only wished they could be me. I convinced myself haters were everywhere.

At the next pledge meeting, I came down hard. I told the pledge class that I knew what they thought of me. It didn't matter, but I wanted to clarify one thing. I remember saying, "I may be confident, and yes, you can call me a little bit cocky, but *never* call me conceited." I thought at the time conceited was when you take advantage of others, and honestly, I would never hurt anyone for my personal gain. I have known hurt; that isn't something I want to put out in the world.

I assured myself that wasn't me. I had more little brothers than anyone in the fraternity, five in total. I was a very giving and caring person. I just let it all go to my head. I wanted to be on top, and in most places in life, I was. I was only trying to help everyone. I wanted them to achieve what I had, to craft a fulfilling life. That is what was on my heart. That is truly what I was trying to do for myself. The problem was my actions just messed it all up. I didn't understand that not everyone was me, nor did they want to be. There is only one Brandon.

Unfortunately, I did not learn my lesson the day the pledge called me to the mat. I didn't even learn it within my college days. I wished I knew at the time how powerful the grip of pride truly was and is. Once it settles inside you, takes its place in your mind and begins to control every move you make, it's nearly impossible to erase. I struggled with these pieces of myself for years. I let little storms rage. What I needed was the exact opposite of pride—humility. Conviction sometimes hurts. A true way of showing humility is through the vulnerability of admitting your mistakes. It wasn't until years later that I was forced to lay my cards on the table and face my reality.

Tools in the Toolbox
Tool #4: Pruning Shears

Two particular quotes come to mind when it comes to this matter. The first, "Inside each of us, there is the seed of both good and evil. It's a constant struggle as to which one will win. And one cannot exist without the other," by Eric Burdon. The other, "Pride is not a threat to God—it is a threat to our relationship with him," by C. S. Lewis. Both are exceptionally on point.

The seed is planted. The fertilizer is down, and the growth has sprouted. As the tree begins to stretch towards the sky, strengthening along the way, there is an important part of the process that cannot be ignored. In the last tool, I explained the importance of why we must fertilize and feed the need. Now, we must look at growth. Growth works on multiple levels.

Think of any given tree. If you do not prune the unruly limbs, the integrity of the foundation can be jeopardized. If the top of the tree becomes too heavy, the base can be uprooted. If the only thing you hear echoing in the background is timber, the entire thing is about to come tumbling down. It takes nutrients, proper fertilization, and care to keep the tree growing.

That care I'm speaking of is known as pruning. You know those little wild, unruly limbs that pop up and suck up the nutrients from the tree? Those are called suckers limbs. If left unattended, they grow wild and steal the life from the stronger, healthier older branches. If the older branches aren't fed, they dry up and eventually fall off.

The ways of the tree can be used in life. We must prune the wild, unruly limbs before they become full-sized branches that steal the life from the foundation and everything you worked to build on top of it.

I didn't realize my limbs had become branches. Big branches filled with pride and greed that worked to suck the life out of the best part of me. I didn't realize my tree was top-heavy and under serious threat of cracking at the base.

What does your tree look like? Are all of your branches stretching towards the beautiful heavens, being filled with all the glorious things that make you shine and grow? Do you have wild growth threatening to become full-sized branches? Are they already there?

Remember every tree can be reshaped, pruned, and given new life. Stay on top of the seed you plant. When you fertilize be careful of the mixture you lay down. Stay grounded. Prune so that your tree stays well-rounded and can fully flourish in the way that God intended. As the quote says, there are seeds of good and evil in us. Which seed will you let win? Have you committed to growing your tree or have you let it grow wild and out of control?

It takes commitment to grow properly. Pick up the shears and cut off anything acting like a sucker. There is too much to lose to allow the wild limbs to become full-sized branches. You now have tool #4, pruning shears, to use to its fullest. Toss it in your toolbox and come along.

Chapter 6
In His Image: A "Model"ed Life

Professor Ed Pilkington's name may not mean much to you, but for me it symbolizes one of the biggest seed planters in my life. As I have mentioned, I began college with the idea of becoming a businessman. Regardless of how fast I wanted to move on that track, I still have to take care of my general requirements. By the time I registered for my freshman semester most of the "desired" extracurricular classes were already full.

With the classes limited, I decided I would take "Introduction to Theater and Dance."

The class wasn't early in the morning, and it was just about the only class that would fit into my class load. I had no idea what to expect. Just like my other general education classes, the first couple sessions of Professor Pilkington's were a general overview of how theater and the selection process of attaining the cast of a play or movie were decided. At this point, I was still wondering how I ended up in this foreign world.

I distinctively remember him standing before the class and describing what it takes to cast the perfect male, female, and villain for any performance. In my best attempt to blend in and hide in the shadows of the back of the room, I pulled my worn-out Tar Heel hat to cover my eyes and tucked my head down, certain I had escaped the professor's glaring eyes. The man had better vision than I was hoping.

He said, "You… in the Carolina hat."

Carolina hat, I thought to myself and sighed. I looked up and saw not only was Pilkington calling me out, so was the entire class. With extreme reluctance, I went down to the front of the class with a few others. Each of us had to state our names and where we were from loud enough that the entire class could hear—particularly those in the back row, which is where I was still longing to be.

Pilkington first wanted to know who should be cast as the leading man. Through that sound, yet sophisticated system of holding his hands over each of our heads, Pilkington asked the class to clap for their choice.

"Brandon?" he announced.

The applause erupted.

He smiled and said, "You are the hero of the play."

At the end of class, Professor Pilkington asked to speak to me. He wanted to know my interest in being on stage, mainly being a part of the cast in the upcoming University play. His words were kind, perhaps gathering I was rather reluctant to even having the conversation.

"I can envision you up there," he pressed.

I appreciated the gesture, but I thanked him and replied, "I am here to be the next great entrepreneur, not an actor."

We parted ways that day. The issue was closed in my mind, but it was far from over in his. I was able to blend in during the second class but by the time the third class rolled around, Professor Pilkington asked me to step into his office.

He explained that he did see something in me, something he doesn't see in many. He asked again if I would consider being a part of the play's ensemble. I listened to his words, halfway tuning him out while I gazed around his office. Dozens of framed photos of past casts were hung in frames. Then there were a few individually framed "star pupils" that caught my eye. One, in particular, was quite fetching.

Hanging in a single frame was one of the most stunning girls I had ever seen. There was something special about her eyes, her smile. I pointed to her photograph and told the good professor that I would do the play if she would do it too.

He quickly smiled and relayed the bad news. She had graduated the year before and was out in Los Angeles modeling, acting, and making a name for herself. Always being quick-witted, I smiled and said, "Well, she was my condition for doing the play. If I can't meet her, then I'm not interested."

He was puzzled, curious as to why she would be the reason that would make me take or not take the role. The answer was simple. Like I had said before she was beautiful. I could see through her smile that her heart was genuine and she had a good spirit. It radiated from her.

Pilkington said, "How do you know all that?"

To which I replied, "The same as you say you can see something in me."

"Touché," he replied, and then told me that he could introduce me at some point when she came home to visit.

It seemed like an empty promise to get me into the play. Thinking I was outwitting the old professor I said, "How will you know when she is coming back to town?"

"Well," he replied, "She is my daughter—Piper. I am sure I will know when she flies in for a visit."

Talk about your heart dropping, your mouth going dry, and your face becoming a lovely shade of beet red. My foot was so firmly in my mouth I wasn't sure I had the strength to limp out of the man's office. From the sheer embarrassment, I had to close the subject quickly.

I said, "I am sorry. I'm just not interested."

The subject was dead.

I had no idea that the seed had been planted and that even though I said no then, that wouldn't mean I would say no later.

Fast-forward four years. I was in my last year as an undergraduate. By now I was hitting the gym daily. One afternoon I was working out and who walks in the door, but none other than the girl in the frame—Piper Pilkington. I couldn't believe my eyes. She was even more beautiful in person than in that picture in her father's office.

A friendship was formed immediately. After a couple of weeks, I realized we had enough in common that I asked her to dinner. Of course, in the back of my mind all I could think of was how awkward it would be to see her father again. I was worried he may rat me out about our conversation in his office four years earlier.

I decided to beat him to the punch. During our first date, I mentioned I knew her father, that I had taken his

class my freshman year. She smiled and laughed. I asked
her what was so funny, and she said she already knew all
about my time in her father's class. I asked how. How in
the world did she know? I felt like an idiot.

She eased my upset by explaining that after meeting
me at the gym she had gone home and gave a detailed
description of the boy she had met. To which her father
responded with, "Sounds as though you finally met
Brandon Russell."

The same redness I felt in her father's office touched
my face at the dinner table. Thankfully Piper found the
whole fiasco endearing. It set off a six-month relationship
that ended when the West Coast called her back. With a
new show and an opportunity beckoning her back to
advance her dreams, I knew we were moving in different
directions, or so I thought.

I tell you these moments with Piper not to rekindle or
talk about old flames, but merely to say that like her father,
Piper planted a big seed in my life too.

She was accomplished and versed in the modeling
world. She knew the ways of L.A. and felt like I belonged.
I didn't feel comfortable with making that kind of decision
at the time, I was a businessman—period; there was no way
around it. Eventually, as a way to pacify her relentless
push, I went and visited with an agency. Little did I know
that they would want to sign me on immediately. Suddenly,
it felt right, and I jumped. A new era in my life began.

Two days—that's all it took to be booked on my first
modeling job after signing my name on the line. It was a

Christmas commercial for Belk, a clothing department store that specializes in modern southern style. You know, sweater vest, brightly colored polos, and rugged plaid shirts with a nice pair of trousers. I sat on a sofa by a roaring fire and pushed their latest line. The experience was incredible. I liked it so much I knew this was what I wanted to do.

But first I had to tell my father.

"What happened to being a businessman?" he asked. I could tell he wasn't thrilled.

It was an honest question. I had just finished school. He had spent five years' worth of his hard-earned money on tuition. He questioned my intentions, as he should have. In his mind, why did I go to college if all I wanted to do was lollygag around the world looking good in front of a camera? As always, my father was levelheaded with this sudden shift of events, but still, he knew if I didn't get into the business world while my degree was still relevant, those five years really would be a waste of both time and money. I assured him I would be using my education to the fullest. I wasn't necessarily advertising and marketing a particular product, but in the end, I was marketing me. In my mind, it made me a threat in the modeling world. I had the skills and knowledge to make strategic choices. It empowered me to hold myself to a different standard and not take every job that would be tossed my direction. If nothing else, owning my own business was my plan B.

Regardless of his concern and questions, there was one thing my father never did. He never once discouraged my brother and me. He never told us we couldn't do something our hearts desired. He never told me that modeling was an outlandish idea or a waste of time. He only nodded his head and supported me even if he questioned my motives. That is what a great father does. The confirmation of support came the day I saw my comp card in his briefcase.

In my heyday, models carried 5x8 comp cards; you can liken them to a business card, essentially. The front of the card listed the model's stats under the best headshot or photo. Mine read: 6'2, 186 lbs., brown eyes and dark brown hair, 32" waist, size 11 shoe, and 42L chest. Directors knew everything they needed to know by that combination of numbers. On the back, a collage of four pictures showed the diversity and skill of that particular model. The card was ever-changing, updated with each new season and market you entered.

I found out later that he carried my comp cards with him when he visited clients. He showed everyone who was willing to take a look—especially the ladies to which he would respond that I got all my looks from him. I still laugh thinking about him saying that with his patented smirk. He was proud of me, and that is all a child can ask of their parent.

As work ramped up, the standards I held myself to were still in the forefront. My faith still reigned supreme. My experience in this fast-moving, ever-changing, high-energy lifestyle was different than some I know. I walked the straight and narrow. I never allowed comments to mess with my head, but I was also not told I was too thin, or fat, or not this or that.

I suppose I'm lucky in that way because it does happen. I wasn't drawn into a lifestyle of debauchery. I went to work. I worked hard on the sets I was employed on and went back to living the life I had designed for myself. I was out to prove that there was more to the modeling industry than others thought. That isn't to say I didn't experience uncomfortable situations.

At age twenty-five, I was up for a major contract. I knew the brand well. Everyone in America knew their name at the time. The clothing store is still thriving today. Therefore, I will keep the name anonymous—though, I must say, some of the luster has worn off its appeal.

Regardless, if I landed this campaign, my career would receive a huge kick-start and there would be no looking back.

I was excited about this opportunity. Things were shaping up for me. That is until I stood before the photographer and was asked a series of very pointed questions.

Starting with, "Will you take your shirt off?"

I was in shape. I had nothing to hide. This was a standard, especially with more physique-based modeling, but the questions that followed, the prying into a guy who they assumed was seventeen, at the oldest nineteen, because of how young I looked and hoped that I was naïve, set my insides screaming.

I had long accepted the fact that in the industry of beauty my body would promote and sell products. I never had a moral issue with this fact, but I did have standards as to what I would be willing to show, how far I would go, and how those images would be used.

The director wanted both another model and me to drop our pants and get down to just our underwear. We were both similar in age and body type and did as instructed, because again this wasn't uncommon—no red flags were sent up just yet. It was the next question of, 'Now, will you please drop your underwear and let me see your backside," that everything inside me began to scream no.

I hadn't been told that the campaign wasn't really about clothing; it was about our backsides. I had two choices: do as directed and make a buck or I could leave standing on my morals.

I refused, but that only made the mental warfare the photographer had packed in his case turn up to full force.

"Are you not comfortable with your body?" he asked.

"I'm extremely comfortable with my body," I replied.

"Apparently not if you won't let others see it," he shot back. "If you were comfortable with your body, you would not have a problem with other people seeing it."

His words were laughable. I wasn't an innocent, gullible kid that was looking for anything to build me up, to gain an ounce of confidence by selling myself short. I already knew where I stood.

I replied quickly, "I am extremely comfortable with my body because I can see how badly you want to see it."

He was the type you are warned against when entering into this world. He threatened me saying I would never

65

make it in this industry. In the end, this was nothing but a mind game to manipulate the insecure to sell their bodies to the world.

The other model was also a Christian. He agreed with my way of thinking and together our higher moral ground led us out of that room with our heads held high and my confidence beaming. There would be other calls—calls that did not lead me into a trap that I may never find my way out of. Those invitations did come in my career in the way of Guess, Ralph Lauren, other Belk ads, and fitness magazines. All I could do was continue to work both professionally and on myself, trust in God that he had given me the proper foundation to survive the sinful possibilities placed in my path, and keep my feet on the ground.

In a way, I was lucky. My upbringing instilled a sense of confidence that many around me were still seeking externally. My foundation kept me from needing to hear how beautiful I was every day. I knew there were others better than I. I knew that I wouldn't be selected for every job I was sent on. The self-absorption and self-love I experienced were nothing compared to the game of Charades that my brothers tossed at me on the fraternity floor. Observation is an amazing teacher. The most important lesson I learned was that the worst part of conceit is the notion that it leads to self-doubt when someone isn't always expressing that you are the center of the universe. Compliments do not breed confidence. That comes from a place no man can provide.

Beauty fades. We age. There has to be something more to life. When the good feeling and taste for the ego-driven world in which I lived began to wear on me, I was offered a new experience. Models for Christ was a Christian organization filled with some of the most beautiful people in the world who stood for something more than self-absorption and the mighty dollar.

They were planters of the mustard seed. This weekly devotional Bible study became a tremendous part of my life.

Here I was among friends, not only personally but in the industry, like-minded soldiers for God. By the standard of the group, the faithful did not do drugs, on the whole, were non-drinkers, and walked the walk while talking the talk. Our hands and feet went into communities and offered service between the flash of lights and the roll of the camera. Here was the 'model'ed life of Christ I yearned to create.

My boundaries continued to be tested. There were times I was served with a heaping serving of humble pie. Not that I didn't deserve it, trust me. Satan kept finding a way of sneaking in and trying his best to create havoc and further test my ability to keep my feet on God's foundation.

An offer came that would have been impossible for most to resist; I said most.

The contract would have made my entire year. It would have given me a sense of comfort to know I wouldn't have to worry about the light bill, but the cost was high. Security meant selling the coolness of a cigarette.

There were guidelines in place, I'm certain there still is, that ruled the standards of all alcohol and cigarette ads that used models. Legally, no one under twenty-five is allowed to sell this lifestyle or image. I mention this because these standards are in place to protect the younger generation from being influenced by a younger model participating in these activities. I was over the age limit but still looked much younger than my age. The ad executives knew I would appeal to a younger crowd. Of course, they would never admit to that, but that was the reason why I was being presented the offer. As a non-smoker, it seemed ridiculous to push something I hadn't ever even held in my hand, let alone put in my mouth.

The question came again. Which would it be: morals or security?

My morals won. I wouldn't be able to sleep well at night if I was the cause of a single child picking up a cigarette and becoming hooked. Not to say I find smoking morally wrong. What I am saying is, I believe we have a moral responsibility to not support something that could harm someone else—especially a child.

Every choice I made came down to my responsibility to not only God, but myself and my community. I will never forget when I had to explain to my agent, who was frankly baffled, that I did not want to do the campaign. For him, it came down to money. To me, it came down to duty. I told him I didn't want the money. If I held tight and chose the higher ground, the amount of money being offered, plus some, would come back to me somehow. He quickly said,

"How do you know that making two or three times this amount would come back?"

I laughed and explained that I never said it was guaranteed that money would come, but by blessing others in their protection I will be blessed in other ways. It may be that I am given the most incredible wife to create a beautiful and solid marriage, or that I have healthy children.

Blessings come in all forms and shapes; it doesn't have to be monetary. This ad, its content, wasn't the seed I wanted to plant in others' minds.

Even beauty has an ugly side. It comes down to where do you let your light shine and where do you let the darkness take over?

Tools in the Toolbox
Tool #5: BE*lieve* in YOU*rself*

Stand up. Go ahead. Find the closest mirror. What do you see? Are you happy with your reflection? If you're not, push all the negatives aside and focus on something you love about yourself. Now, think of another positive. And another, until all of those negatives are flipped on their head.

Now, peer into the mirror. Stare into your own eyes and become mesmerized by the amazing soul and person you are on the inside. Once that image is firmly locked in your mind, slowly start focusing on your physical presence once more. No matter what the outside world sees, you are absolutely perfect. You are beautiful!

With complete conviction, repeat after me: I am perfect in God's image. I am beautiful!

Go ahead. I'll wait.

You must believe in yourself and not be afraid to BE YOU. The you that stands firmly on a solid foundation. God believed in you when you were created. Your inner and outward beauty was his gift not only for you to enjoy but for the world to benefit from too. If you trip into sowing the negative seed of poor self-image, it steals the beauty God created you in. Those negatives only make you afraid to allow yourself to shine! Be you! No one else can or ever will be as unique as YOU!

When using God's gifts, set boundaries. As I explained in this chapter, I stood firm, never crossing the moral line that would have stolen the glory of the gifts God gave me. Once you cross the moral line, it's easier to do it the second time. After a few instances of lowering your morals, the morals begin to blur and fade. I refused to be that person when asked.

Manipulation is a nasty tactic. It can break down the walls of confidence and moral integrity by preying on insecurities. If you stand on your beliefs, no one can break those walls or shake your foundation. I believed in ME! You must believe in YOU! This same thought goes for the opportunities that will come in the future. An opportunity may sound rewarding and enticing but at the heart of the so-called chance is a fork in the road that may cause you pain and eternal damage if you turn left when you should have turned right. Is your moral compass properly calibrated?

Never allow that compass to be affected by the magnetic charge of temptation and greed.

Money and material things come and go as quickly as external beauty fades; your moral compass should not.

Are you still looking in the mirror? Here is another important question. Are your actions worthy of being called a role model? You never know who is watching your every move. A friend could value your opinion and the way you choose to live your life. Perhaps a co-worker views you as a guide to which they direct their moral compass. Have you thought about the example you are leaving for your child, a relative, or even the man at the grocery store?

If I allowed myself to fall into the temptation of money by taking a job selling cigarettes and alcohol I would not be a shepherd—a proper role model. I would be leading others into a place I did not nor ever will place any amount of value. A model is chosen because of acceptance, the power of persuasion, and the ability to make people feel and desire something, whether it is clothing, a lifestyle, or even a cigarette.

When I was questioned why I refused to model in ads that weren't in line with my compass, I knew my moral standing would come back tenfold in another way through God's grace. I am a firm believer in doing good for others. That if you stand strong in your beliefs and faith, in the end you are rewarded with immeasurable blessings.

Are you standing in his image? Are you living a model life? Start with the inside and project your brilliance out into the world. You now have tool #5, Believe in You, to use to its fullest. Toss it in your toolbox and come along.

Chapter 7
Judging a Book by Its Cover

You learn more about life through whom you surround yourself with than any lecture or textbook any school has to offer. It's those extraordinary people that shape your overall view in life if you are privileged enough to meet someone like Ruth Ellen Weems.

During my first summer in college, I decided to settle down in Boone, North Carolina, and get a job for the summer. I've told you about what led to my change of career, but I would be remiss if I didn't tell you this exceptionally important part of my life story. In fact, it has a lot to do with who I am today. It's funny how you are chugging along in life, and an opportunity comes up that you don't even realize will make a lifelong impact upon you.

Settling in, I found this little hair salon, ventured in for a haircut, and got to know the owner. Her name was Delores, but we called her Purple D because everything in the salon was purple. I mean everything, the walls, the combs, hair dryer—you name it—all were a shade of purple. I stopped by every other week to check in and say hello. A friendship sparked between Purple D and me. Valuing her hard work as a business owner and our friendship, I sent my fraternity brothers and friends to her to help build her clientele. I may or may not have told the pledges that they *had* to see her, but trust me, once they stepped foot in that purple-clad salon they were happy they followed my instruction. Delores was a knock-out.

As our friendship grew, she asked me what I was doing for work. With my love for the outdoors and working with my hands, I had taken a job with a landscape company and was basking in the summer sun between edging and mowing. Delores felt I needed to be doing more, and mentioned that a woman at the Blowing Rock Country Club was looking for someone to help around her home.

The minute she said her name, Ruth Ellen Weems, my wheels began to turn—even Ruth Ellen's name seemed stately and classic. Immediately I thought to myself, Blowing Rock Country Club is the nicest country club I have ever laid my eyes on. The money and the snooty pretentious rolled through my mind. I laughed and said, "I am not going to help some rich country club socialite by fetching her more sugar and crumpets for her hot tea and answer the door like a butler."

Delores smiled back and replied, "Well, I don't know if that is what she wants, she just asked if I would ask around to find someone."

In honor of Delores and my friendship, I set up a meeting with Ruth Ellen to interview for the so-called butler's job. I got there expecting to be greeted by a pretentious woman who truly expected me to wait on her hand and foot. Talk about learning not to judge a book by its cover; when Ruth Ellen came to the door, my pre-conceived notions were washed away by the most down-to-earth, generous, and kind soul I have yet to meet, next to my own mother of course. I was blown away by how nice and humble she was, and for lack of a better word, normal.

My job would be simple. She needed help opening the house up for the summer. Ruth Ellen is from Florida, and I quickly came to learn that it is fairly common for the residents in Blowing Rock to come north to the mountains in May and stay until October. I couldn't blame them—it is the perfect scenario—avoid the tourist and crowding of the summer beaches during the summer, soak up the marvelous views of mountains and the fresh air, then return to Florida before the snow touches the top of the peaks.

While the Weems were away, the house was closed for six months, and it needed to be cleaned, aired out, and freshened up a bit. Ruth Ellen wanted more than a cleaning crew, she needed someone to pull the furniture from the walls, and clean the stunning place from the ceilings to the splendid tongue-and-groove white pine floors. The job was simple enough and I took it.

I set to work immediately. It took four days to clean every wall, floor, and piece of furniture within the Weems's home. When I told Ruth Ellen I was ready for the next task, she was shocked.

"How did you do the whole house already?" she asked. "I thought it would take at least two or three weeks."

I had left my job with the landscaping company to help Ruth Ellen. I couldn't imagine what I was going to do for the rest of the summer. That's when Ruth Ellen began to spread the word that I was available to help care for other families' homes. Little did I know that Ruth Ellen was helping me turn my summer job into a budding business. Eight families later, I was doing odds and ends for anyone who called. She introduced me to Mather, the owner of a fine dining restaurant called Twigs, and I started waiting tables too. What started as a supposed three-week project grew into a lifelong relationship that is more like family than friend.

The Weems decided to move into a new home, and I was there to help her through the process. Soon, I was there three times a week, and the lessons I learned were and still are invaluable. Because of her I was making great money during college, and I decided I wanted to buy a new car—at least new to me. I settled on a used Range Rover. The SUV was in great shape and was perfect for the snow-covered mountains of Boone. Ruth Ellen, being wise and twice my age, questioned my motives of buying such a flashy automobile.

"Why do you need such an expensive car, Brandon?" she asked.

I reassured her I was getting an excellent deal, and I could afford it.

"Sure," she said, "but I'm talking more about the maintenance. That car is a lot to care for."

While I respected her opinion, valued it is more correct, I didn't listen and slapped my money down and drove away with a sweet Range Rover of my very own. It made me feel good to get into that car. While it wasn't so much about status, it was mine, something I had done on my own and it didn't hurt that it did have an ounce of flash.

I should have paid more attention to Ruth Ellen. She was never one to show off, never boasted about what she had even though she had more than plenty, and she chose to drive a very practical Chevy Tahoe. It was brand new, of course, but a Chevy just the same. The Weems never had a worry when it came to monetary matters and I was just a college student who, like most, had to make sure I was making ends meet. Ruth Ellen could buy a new car every day of the month if she wanted to, but she didn't. I was naïve. I still had so much to learn about life from Ruth Ellen.

Ruth Ellen took me under her wing. Her husband John is just as humble and giving as his wife. He is also quite honestly the smartest and nicest man I've ever met. He is a man among men, and was also there to give me great wisdom in a time when I was still pouring my foundation. They quickly became my second set of parents while I was at school. I still to this day call them Momma and Papa Blowing Rock.

It was here where I learned that life isn't about the cover of the book, it's about what's written on the inside pages. One morning the phone rang. Ruth Ellen answered the line to find her housekeeper in Florida was in distress. She was caring for her ill mother and had to purchase more medicines than her salary could afford. She wanted an advance on her earnings to care for her family. Without a second thought or even another question, Ruth Ellen told her not to worry the money would be there by the morning. Pulling out her checkbook, Ruth Ellen wrote a check not for the amount her housekeeper asked for, but instead, it was for three times what was needed. She wrote a note that read something to the nature of, "This is not an advance. I just want you to take care of your family." She handed it to me and asked me to go to the post office immediately and overnight the funds. She didn't have to do that. She could have said no, or she could have said this is an advance and it will be deducted from your salary. She could have even written out only the amount requested, but instead, she gave because that is what you do in life.

You care for and love those in need. It was then I realized that I would never not help when I was needed and I would never allow anyone to take advantage of my momma Blowing Rock. There were those that tried.

Ruth Ellen wanted a fresh look around the house. She hired a designer. He pulled up and began to unload dozens of small items. He randomly placed them throughout the house and when he was done, he gave her a bill that was in the thousands. I was shocked by the fee and knew the designer was trying to exploit the location of the home and Ruth Ellen. I asked her to go upstairs and proceeded to remove all the items the designer had brought into the house. The home was already filled with amazing things. I moved key pieces into new locations and called her back down. To her surprise, all the decorator's items were gone, but she loved what I had done. I stuffed everything the designer brought in the closet and told her to call him and have it all picked up.

You know what a good person someone is when you mess up, and all they do is laugh and graciously pardon your inexperience. Once Ruth Ellen asked me to take the rugs out and hang them over the railing outside. They needed a good beating to pound the dust out. While I was out there pounding away, I noticed that the fringe was starting to darken from how dirty they were. I quickly went inside to mix up the perfect concoction to surprise and clean them for Ruth Ellen. It seemed logical at the time that when you do the laundry, you use Clorox to get things back to their brilliant white. I mixed up a bucket of three parts Clorox to one part water.

While I knew the rugs were exquisitely woven masterpieces, I had no clue of their monetary value. Had I known, I wouldn't have dared even touch the things without white gloves. But there I was scrubbing the fringe of these insanely with bleach. The fringe shined a brilliant white when I was done. I was thrilled I was able to restore them back to the natural thread, or so I thought. Of course, you can already guess what happened. After the rugs had dried, I placed them back in the house. When Ruth Ellen came home, she was so excited over how I had restored the beautiful carpets back to their original brilliance. I was happy my surprise worked out so well.

Well, it did until about a week later while I was vacuuming I looked down to see there wasn't a tassel of the fringe left. The only thing remaining was a small nub where they were once tied. In disbelief, I called Ruth Ellen down and showed her the problem. I had never had a rug do that before.

Ruth Ellen looked down and said, "Brandon, what did you clean those with?"

After I explained my miracle concoction of bleach and water, Ruth Ellen just laughed.

Obviously, the bleach ate through the delicate fibers completely ruining the fringe. I felt awful.

While others would have sent me out to look for another job, that wasn't Ruth Ellen. Her being the generous, loving soul she is didn't even yell. She didn't dock my pay. She didn't even tell me how stupid my actions were, which I did deserve. Instead, it was lesson learned, and I got a lesson on the proper proportion of bleach to water ratios. That was the first time I really remember how grace felt. Now I just laugh at my inexperience. I certainly know how to take care of a rug now.

The Weems moved one more time before I graduated. This time they moved into the most amazing house in the country club. I literally could have died in this home and felt my life was complete. It was stunning. Ruth Ellen truly has a calling for making homes look and feel amazing inside. It was there that I slowly developed my abilities in design. I learned so much about maintaining a home.

Some of my most valuable life lessons as an adult were formed inside the Weems's homes.

When I think back, I cannot imagine my life without them, and yet, I almost allowed my judgment of a person I hadn't even met take away my opportunity to grow in life. Both Ruth Ellen and John showed me nothing but grace and guidance, and for that, I will never forget all they have done for me. Nor will I ever forget that you must read the pages of someone's story before you let the cover dictate who they really are.

Tools in the Toolbox
Tool #6: Judgment and Forgiveness
"Do not judge, and you will not be judged. Do not condemn, and you will not be condemned. Forgive, and you will be forgiven."
Luke 6:37

Can you imagine the world without judgment? I can, but it doesn't exist. I love Luke 6:37. It's the true golden rule of life. Do not judge, and you will not be judged. It seems simple enough, yet hard to practice because it is built into the fabric of our society. I know I'm guilty.

We are taught at an early age to be careful and wary of strangers. We are told not to talk to people we do not know. We are told there is a good and bad side of town. We are taught these rules of life because our parents and guardians are trying to develop a sense of wrong and right, but at the same time, it gives us the first taste of judgment. It's these ideals that shape into subconscious judgments of those who live by a different set of standards. This is how we continue to allow our character to build a defense around ourselves.

We all know the American standard for justice: innocent before proven guilty. While it may be difficult to make every decision with this simple idea in mind, it's something I try to remember. Think about it, if I hadn't met Ruth Ellen, I would have lost out because of my prejudgment. Instead, I went, learned, and found power in the lasting examples I was taught in Boone.

The Bible teaches that it is not our place as Christians to pass judgments. It also says as Christians when these judgments are made that we must ask for forgiveness. That leads me to a very powerful part of judgment and that is forgiveness.

There is not a living soul on this earth that hasn't experienced pain in some form or another. The simple fact that we are human begs for us to experience this sadly needed notion in our lives.

I say needed because without pain we cannot know forgiveness. When speaking in terms of judging someone, this action creates pain, not only for the person being judged, but the judge themselves. As we were forgiven of our sins, we must understand that without this tool we are unable to live a full life. Forgiveness is a gift, not only for the person who caused hurt but also for ourselves.

This is the one tool I beg you to keep close, use often, and never take for granted. The act of forgiveness is not only letting go of the hate and hurt you feel in your heart, but it also releases you from holding back. Think about someone that has hurt you. Do you hold a grudge? Have you refused to offer forgiveness? I bet those emotions of hurt, doubt, and pain sneak up on you when you are least expecting them. The best way to rid yourself of this burden is to forgive. I'll be the first to admit that I'm still working on mastering this tool. Forgiveness doesn't always come easy, but it comes.

In all the ways God forgives us, we must learn to forgive situations that occur in life. It's so important that we learn from our judgments. What could seem good may be bad. What looks bad may be a blessing in disguise. By removing the lens of judgment and acting with a forgiving heart, these choices are easier to discern when they appear.

I asked you moments ago, is there a situation or person you need to forgive? Try to think of forgiveness like this; it must be created. It doesn't appear on its own. It's something you have to work to create. By taking action, we foster forgiveness.

If you are in need of this healing tool try these simple steps:

Reflect on the situation. Do you need to offer forgiveness to the person and mend the rifts, or is it best to forgive internally and let go?

Apologize for your contribution to the problem.

Consider the fact that we are all imperfect human beings.

Release the burdens you carry in all situations.

Don't avoid people, instead, embrace them. Not every situation is going to lead to hurt.

Set a new path. Understand that one rough road doesn't mean that life will always be filled with judgment and upset. Stand firm on your foundation in faith and move forward with the mighty forgiveness God gave to us.

The impact of forgiveness is far-reaching. Are you ready to let go of the preconceived ideas that do not serve you or others? Are you ready to heal yourself and the situations that beg you to take note? Do you have the power to harness forgiveness? Do you know how to take off the lens of placing a verdict on someone who isn't on trial? That answer is yes. Forgiveness doesn't make you weak, it makes you so incredibly strong. Allow yourself to use only sound judgment, it makes you incredibly strong too. You owe that to yourself. If you are ready to use superior judgment in all facets of life only with good motivations, and you are ready to put an ounce of forgiveness in everything you do, then you have tool #6, judgment and forgiveness, ready to be used. Toss it in your toolbox and come along.

Chapter 8
Spared: September 11, 2001
"So do not fear, for I am with you; do not be dismayed, for I am your God. I will strengthen you and help you; I will uphold you with my righteousness."
Isaiah 41:10

The title of this chapter may already have your attention, and rightfully so. September 11, 2001, is a crucial mark in America, in time, in the hearts of so many; it is and will always be a reminder of God's love and plan for me. It's the day He allowed my journey to continue, even if the reason is sometimes elusive. I suppose I should tell you how.

New York City—the center of the universe—The Big Apple, the streets of golden opportunity. It's a place you should go if you are ever in need of being humbled. The sheer size of the smallest building will serve as a reminder of how tiny your presence truly is in this great big world. It's also the epicenter of fashion in the United States, and that is the reason my feet hit the opportunity-lined pavement in 2001.

My modeling career had taken off at home. I was being booked on a regular basis by my agency in Atlanta, Georgia. The money was steady, as was the work, but I thirsted for more. During those days, I met two of my closest friends, Sean Martin and Dennis O'Neil. The pair were also models and were ready to take the fashion world by storm. Each of us brought different aspects to the table and offered no threat to the other, therefore we were the perfect trio.

Dennis had met a stylist that would be out of the country for a month, and she offered her place, rent-free, if he wanted to head to New York and get his feet wet in the major leagues. He had been in New York for a couple of weeks when he called Sean and I up and asked us to join him. A plan was made, and this sounded like the perfect scenario.

Once we arrived, the objective was to visit as many agencies as possible over five short days. We were hoping to get our foot in the door and be signed by the likes of Ford, Wilhelmina, or Next modeling agencies. Our sights were set on the next level of our careers, and honestly, when we arrived, it didn't seem to matter which company would take us. Later it did, but that story will come.

My first day in New York was September 9, 2001. I walked out of LaGuardia Airport with my suitcase in hand and a dream flourishing in my head. Quickly, I jumped in a taxi and set off to meet up with Dennis. I did my best to act cool, not do anything that would let even the most seasoned New Yorker pick up on the fact that I was a tourist, but I was just a good ole' southern boy with my chin up in the air in awe of everything the city had to offer. Just short of a tourist attraction map dangling from my fingers and a street cart hot dog, I reeked of New York City newbie.

Once I arrived, Dennis told me he had been selected to walk the FUBU fashion show; I arrived just in time to support him as he took to the runway. The excitement still jumps through my veins when I think of that first exposure to the real New York fashion lifestyle. The event was star-studded. A-listers and the modeling world's elite crowded the front of the catwalk. The buzz in the air only churned my desire to delve deeper into this world.

After the show, we went to Eugene's, an exclusive venue that catered to the young, rich, and beautiful crowd. The place is now closed, but it was here I got my first taste of New York City—literally. Here Dennis and I were among the stars and the ladder climbers at a private party hosted by Maxim Magazine in honor of a megastar's birthday. Out of respect and privacy for this star, I'll refrain from using her name, but the story is still important.

As I made my way through the door, she just so happened to be walking over. She greeted me with a warm "hello," and I remember being struck by how nice she was.

I went to the bar to grab a drink and celebrate the amazing night. Yes, by then I had started to drink here and there, but the key was I did so in moderation. I ordered a single bottle of beer. Not one of those fancy twelve dollar beers that scream I've got something to prove, but just a run-of-the-mill, domestic bottle of beer. The bartender looked up, and said, "Ten dollars."

To which I replied, "Oh no, sorry, I just wanted one."

He replied, "Yeah, I heard you. It's ten dollars."

Shocked, I smirked, "Are you kidding me? I have never paid more than three bucks for that beer at home."

All he said was, "Welcome to New York buddy."

I forked over the money in utter disbelief. It was an eye-opening experience, to say the least. It quickly makes you appreciate growing up in a place where money is stretched a bit further. Regardless how much was spent it was still a night to remember.

The next morning Dennis and I hit the streets. I wanted to see everything the city had to offer. First stop, Canal Street. Permanent stores and portable vendors are stacked tightly along the street, each hawking their wares. Most items are highly suspect, but if you are in the market to pick up a fake Rolex and fall into the Manhattan cliché, this is the place to make that happen.

From there, we made our way to Times Square. It struck me while staring up at the massive Jumbotrons and colorful print ads draped over nearly every building that this city is and will always be the center of the universe.

Sean hadn't made it to NYC yet. He was scheduled to arrive just before midnight. Dennis and I killed time that evening, so we hit the gym. Once Sean arrived, the three of us would be ready to knock on doors and try to sell our looks; we wanted to look our very best.

In my downtime, I did what I knew best, and I worked as a personal trainer at a gym. It was a mutually benefiting career; I stayed in shape and was always ready for the next fitness call. My gym membership back home allowed Dennis and I to work out at the World Gym.

After numerous sets and reps between the two of us, we left the gym. We were as physically prepared as we would ever be for the following day. By the time we made

our way through the exit doors, nightfall had arrived.
Shining brightly in the near distance stood New York
City's crown jewel, the World Trade Center. The towers
pushed their beautiful light into the darkened sky. I was in
awe of their presence—the sheer size alone was daunting.

Dennis and I made our way back to the loft and settled
in to wait for Sean. While we waited, the calendar changed
from September 10th to September 11th. Just after midnight,
Sean arrived. The trio was together, and we were ready to
take the world by storm. We made small talk, got our plan
together for the next day, and somewhere in that small
window of time, God saved our lives.

Sean and I had a meeting at Next Model Management,
one block over from the World Trade Center, at nine a.m.
We planned to get up around seven and have breakfast at
the Windows on the World restaurant at eight a.m.
Windows on the World was at the top of Building One, the
North Tower, inside The World Trade Center. It would be a
unique New York experience, one that would create a
memory for a lifetime and something that would start the
day off right. With the plans settled, the conversation
changed.

Sean and I were believers, followers of Christ. Dennis
wasn't so sure. Being the child of an American father and a
Korean mother, he grew up in two different religions. Now
that he was old enough to make his own decisions, he
wasn't sure what stance he took on the subject of faith.

I cannot recall how we got onto the subject of God, but
somehow we did. Dennis joined in, asking questions about

our beliefs, about God, and how religion worked in our lives. His queries spurred on a conversation that lasted for hours. We wanted to arm him with the facts, give him insight into our view of God, but we simply did not know that if those questions hadn't been asked, things would be so very different.

I remember climbing into bed around four a.m. Three hours of sleep wouldn't be much, but our plans remained the same. It's true that even the best plans sometimes get changed. All three of us slept passed the alarm. There would be no breakfast that morning at the top of the towers. I would be lucky to make it on time for my appointment at Next Model Management. The agency was close by but still it would be a stretch.

I jumped into the shower unaware of the events taking place up the road, unaware that my phone was ringing frantically in the next room. I was blocks away from the towering presence of the Twin Towers and I was completely unaware of the chaos taking place on the streets.

The first Boeing 767 jet plane struck the North Tower at 8:46 a.m. between the 93rd and 98th floors. I was supposed to be just a few floors above, minding the views of the New York City skyline and eating breakfast. The South Tower was struck shortly after that at 9:03 a.m.

I picked up the phone after I got out of the shower. A girl I was dating at the time had called many times during that short shower. Here she was calling again. Her first words were, "Thank God you are alive."

I had no idea what she meant. Of course, I was alive. Our schedules had been off, she was traveling, and so was I. I figured she was worried about my safety because we hadn't had much communication over those last few days. Her next words still ring in my ears.

"We are under attack."

Silence.

I still had no concept that the same towers I marveled at less than twelve hours before would be coming down before my eyes in a matter of minutes. As she spoke the words that the towers had been hit, I flipped on the television. Channel 36 New York was the only station we were able to pick up. The majority of the signals were broadcasted off the top of the towers at that time. In real time, in New York City, on the fifth floor of an apartment in Soho, I watched the first building start to fall, and then I felt it.

There would be no modeling contracts secured that day. Our focus shifted as did the rest of the country and the world. Dennis, Sean, and I rushed towards the towers. We needed to help. While many fled, many ran towards the wreckage too. We had to do something. We felt helpless, but there was one thing we also felt, thankful to be alive. Had Dennis not asked those questions about God we wouldn't have been rushing towards the building, we would have been lucky to be alive amongst the wreckage, smoke, and flames.

Here in the busiest city in America, it was almost as if time stood still. The streets were covered in gray ash and dust for miles. The familiar sounds of car horns and taxis being hailed were gone. Life was different in the hours that followed.

I knew my parents would surely be panicked after watching the news. The first thought would naturally be: was I alive. Phone and cellular service were spotty, at best. In the fashion my father had taught me, I made Dennis and Sean write down my parents' number on their palm as I took theirs. The first person who was able to make contact would instruct their parent to call the other parents to let them know we were okay. It took hours but finally we got through. It just so happened I was the one who was able to reach my mom first. She was able to call and tell the other mothers that their sons were alive. I cannot imagine the panic they all felt. I'm sure it was something close to what we were experiencing walking the streets.

We tried to help, hand out water, give blood, anything, but those jobs were all filled. I remember sitting inside a small pizzeria that had remained open. We watched a mother and daughter who were clean, unlike so many of us, rush towards a man covered from head to toe in gray soot. The three grabbed each other in a long, deep embrace. This was the spirit of the world coming together before our eyes, an unforgettable and sacred family moment where this family was reunited with their husband and father after hours of gut-wrenching uncertainty.

If you were alive that fateful day, you have a story. It's a place in history that everyone knows what they were doing and what transpired in the hours to follow. Two thousand six hundred six people lost their lives just a few blocks away from me that day and the days that followed. Still, I was spared.

It's funny how God works. Why we were not in that building, why God chose to keep me, Dennis, and Sean on this earth, I still do not know. The answer has not fully shown itself. Perhaps it is to share my experiences and help draw others to faith, in the same way we tried to do for Dennis on September 10th. Perhaps it is for a reason that I won't know until my final days on this earth, but whatever it is, I was spared.

God was there with me in those early morning hours. He was among the questions the night before. He was there when my eyes did not open when the alarm clock called me to wake. I undoubtedly know He was inside those towers too. I know he was with those who were called home and those who would be forever changed. He was there as he will always be.

Our plans were forever changed. Instead of shaking hands and taking photos for talent scouts we were seeking a way home. It took three days but finally we were able to catch a crowded train home.

Our focus had to be shifted. In April of the next year, we took another leap of faith. Sean and I, along with another friend, moved to New York City in hopes of creating what we were seeking in September. I went up with an agency that was hoping to represent me. No formal agreements had been signed yet, but it was a promising lead. I found my way into iconic fashion photographer,

Steven Meisel's studio. I was there for what the industry calls a "go see." Photography studios across the city invited models, at set times, to stop in, with the purpose of possible bookings in the future.

Immediately I was asked which agency I was there with. I explained I was brought in by a particular agency, but I had not yet decided whether or not I would sign with them. The assistant asked me to wait a moment. When she returned, she told me I needed to be a Wilhelmina model. She had called Tom, the booker at Wilhelmina, and I needed to go directly over and see him. I knew the name, Wilhelmina. Anyone in the modeling world did, but I had no idea what a big deal it was for me to leave the go see and walk through the agency's doors with an appointment waiting.

I rushed to the subway as quickly as my legs would carry me. Between the excitement pulsing through my veins and the fury of the train barreling along the tracks, I was in awe. This felt like it was *my* moment. Stepping through doors of the most prominent modeling agency in the world, I could not believe I was shaking hands with Tom.

I was offered full representation. My dreams were coming true. I called my agency back in Atlanta, unsure what to do. They were ecstatic. While I knew I should have signed the contract right then, I still had a meeting at Ford Modeling Agency to honor. I left Tom and his contract waiting while I honored my commitment. A contract was offered at Ford too. It came with a catch, however. I was young-looking at the time, despite already being well into my mid-twenties. Ford casts models in different divisions based solely on their ages. I knew I was too baby-faced at the time to land work amongst thirty- and forty-year-olds. It felt like I would never be able to work in the way I wanted to. I left and signed the contract with Wilhelmina.

My plans may have been uprooted in September. The ground of my foundation was shaken because my grander dreams were placed on hold, but certainly not for long. Things happened in the correct time; who knows what would have happened if September 11th hadn't happened the way it did. There is a host of scenarios that could have played out, but all of them were in God's hands. It doesn't matter the date on the calendar, this still remains true.

Tools in the Toolbox
Tool #7: All in God's Timing

I'm sure you have heard the saying, "Timing is everything." Or what about, "Being in the right place at the right time?" While I couldn't find who originally spoke those words, I wish I could thank them for such sage advice.

In today's world, we have all succumbed to the convenience and ease of using our GPS or phones when we are in need of direction. Have you noticed that when the destination pulls up there is almost always more than one path to end up in the same place? Some routes may take longer, but the ride is sometimes more enjoyable. Others are "faster," but the traffic is always a mess. The point is, there is always more than one road to get to where you are going, and sometimes, even the unpaved streets or the ones with more potholes than you can imagine are necessary.

I think about my life now and each road I took to get here. What if I had taken the bait during Professor Pilkington's class? If I had started acting and modeling then, I would never have taken the longer road to get to where I am today. I would have missed all the valuable leadership skills I gained throughout my fraternity and campus positions. Even if I did experience a few bumps in the road during those days, they were worth every ding. The short route to where I am now may not have been laden with the same character-building forks in the road. I was in the right place when I was called to the front of the class, but the timing wasn't right.

On September 11, 2001, God's perfect timing kept me safe from danger and most likely, death. With my eyes closed and ears turned off to the sound of the alarm clock, I was in the right place at the right time. I still do not know why or what God's reasoning was for sparing me from being at the top of the North Tower when the first plane hit, but there is a reason. I choose to believe he saved me to honor and share his word and mercy. I was given another day to be a seed planter. Another reason may reveal itself somewhere down the road, and should that day come I will welcome it with open arms.

There is another aspect of my time in New York I feel should be addressed too. With the events of the 11th, I was unable to fulfill the very reason I was in the city to begin with. A part of me plays the old *what if* game. What if I had gone to that nine o'clock appointment and the door was slammed in my face? What then? What if I knocked on a thousand doors and behind each door was a no? What then? Would I be the man I am today? The answer is probably not.

Things could have been different. In the wake of the events, I was forced to return to Atlanta where I was living at the time. I never once viewed those days as a lost opportunity. Instead, I went back, chased my goals, readjusted my dream, and made the move back when God placed the right timing on my heart.

Timing is *EVERYTHING*.

There is another part I want to address, and that is, rejection is God's protection. Think about those words— rejection is God's protection. They're powerful, aren't they?

Have you ever been rejected? I know I have been. I bet you felt confused, lost, upset, challenged; there is a host of words that could take up this entire page if I went on, but have you considered that you were rejected because God was protecting you?

God's timing is perfect in everything he does. So if you applied for your dream job and you didn't land it, think about why? Is it because you weren't good enough? Probably not.

Is it because you didn't try hard enough? Probably not. It could be because God knows what is over the horizon. Your vision only allows you to see up to the horizon. Peripheral vision allows you to see left and right. We are simply unable to know and see what lies beyond the horizon, but God sees all. He knows whether there are clear skies or storms ahead. For example, the job you were hoping to get may look great on the surface, but what lies over the horizon is they only have ninety days to keep their doors open. You are being brought in to be their saving grace, but in the end, nothing could have changed their course. Think about the tornado that would whirl through everything you have built for yourself. It's scary, right?

This doesn't only apply to work situations. It could be that new car or truck you really wanted but at this time it can't be yours because the bank won't cover the loan. God knows what you can or cannot afford. It would be a shame to find the repo man on the horizon instead of security. Maybe it's the perfect house, but the price tag is a bit out of your reach. These all may seem like rejections, failures, or upheavals that have you begging for change, but truthfully, it's God's way of steering you through the storm.

Think of it this way: You choose a path on your GPS that seems to be a clear and sturdy shot and the fastest way to reach your destination, but along the way you see the bright orange detour sign that was not on the GPS. It's because it was unaware of the problem ahead. God is your detour sign. Trust him. You may have to go a different way, but he will always get you where you belong.

Have you ever pushed for something despite seeing the warning signs to turn around? One-way road, dangerous curve ahead—your GPS was going crazy—and yet you bypassed the barriers anyways. The storm was massive and mighty, wasn't it?

Whatever it is, God is trying to protect you from the storm. It's so cliché to say ... don't worry, something better will come along, there are better days ahead ... but it's the absolute truth. His timing is perfect, audible, and at times foreseeable if you are willing to wait. Rejection is God's protection!

You now have tool #7, All in God's Timing, is ready to use to its fullest. Toss it in your toolbox and come along.

Chapter 9
Beauty Into Ashes

There are seasons of life—moments where the boy becomes a man, hair turns from dark brown to a slightly lighter shade, where victories and despair touch the soul—and even moments where God comes and tests the core of your faith. What I know now is God even has a way of testing your future.

Things were going well; my face was being splashed all over the place. But things were about to change—rapidly.

Being the hunter he was, my father took off for what was to be a stellar weekend. As he always did, he climbed into a tree and began setting up his tree stand. It had two nail-like prongs that dug into the tree when the correct pressure was applied. Those prongs were the fail-safe for keeping the blind nestled in the tree. He did what he had always done and slightly jumped to make the prongs set. When he did, a weak part of the frame gave way and he started to fall to the ground below.

My father was a survivalist and an even quicker thinker. He quickly wrapped his leg around the tree to slow the momentum of his fall. It worked, but it didn't stop him from hitting the ground. His back struck the earth first. He was okay, nothing was broken, but he didn't escape without injury. His calf muscle was pulled, and his ankle was in pain. By the time he arrived home, his ankle and calf were swollen.

101

He did the usual thing you do when you have a severe sprain or muscle injury. He applied ice regularly, but the swelling wasn't going down. My mom asked him to see a doctor and informed him he only had 72 hours after an incident to seek medical attention if he wanted the insurance to cover the cost. He listened and went in.

The swelling was concerning, and the doctor decided to run some tests. What came back was entirely unexpected. His liver enzyme count was irregular. No one could make the connection between an injured leg and an abnormal count. The next logical step was to do more tests. Then came the call that no one ever wants to receive. The test results showed that my father had signs of cancer.

Cancer.

Impossible, I thought. This man is invincible. They had to be wrong. There is no way cancer could grow and live inside Dennis Russell. He was the strongest, toughest man I knew.

Then fear crept in. There was no way I could walk through this life without him. He was my rock. A man shouldn't be without his father, at least not this early in life.

More extensive tests showed two separate small growths in the liver. This was confirmation. My father had cancer, and he had been fighting it before the fall. This was why the swelling would not resolve on its own. Oddly enough, this sleeping giant wouldn't have been discovered without that misstep in the tree. Now, it was time to look towards healing his body.

A treatment plan was started quickly. It began with tumor ablation. The tumors were small and the good news was it had been caught early. With the treatment plan settled, the goal of the ablation was to destroy the tumors within the liver without removing them. Everyone thought this would be the answer. Treatment would be over, and he could go back to the active life he was living before the fall.

A few months passed. I was in New York full-time and the reports I was getting from home were positive. I settled into a new normal of my father's illness and an exciting strike in my career. A prominent agency in Milan called, and with my signature now on the dotted line, I was headed to Milan for three to six months. This opportunity was a career-changer and a must if I wanted to escalate my portfolio and stature as a top model. This was my chance. I was on top of the world.

I booked a small campaign in Atlanta. The details were falling into place. I would do the campaign on the 6th and 7th of October and head out for Milan on the 11th. I sublet my apartment beginning on October 1st, so I decided to fly into Atlanta early.

The timing worked out perfectly. With my father's birthday coming up on October 3rd and the fact I would not be able to be home for my birthday or the upcoming holidays, these extra days between work would give me a chance to spend time with my parents before I left.

When I arrived at the airport, I was surprised to find my mom waiting for me alone. I brushed it off, thinking my dad probably got busy doing his normal stuff, crafting something striking with his hands or just out mowing the yard and I would see him when we got home. But when I arrived, what I found was a very sick man.

My focus shifted.

Over the next few days, I watched as my dad struggled. He was sluggish at times. His cognitive skills were slipping. I went to my mother privately. I wanted to know if she was seeing what I was. My dad was worse than anyone had let on. She knew I was upset, but my father had asked her not to tell Caleb or me. He didn't want us to worry. We were to carry on with our lives. He didn't want to be a burden, and for me, that was never a thought that entered my mind.

Still, he couldn't see it that way.

It must have been the third day back that I noticed my dad, the sharp-witted man, was starting to take long pauses before answering a question. You would ask him if he wanted more tea and the answer would come over a minute later. Funny, a minute doesn't seem that long but when you are waiting for a simple yes or no, it feels like an eternity.

One of the hardest moments came over a bowl of spaghetti. Dad was slowly twirling his fork trying to catch a few noodles, but as he brought the fork to his lips the noodles slipped off and landed back on the plate. My dad didn't notice. The metal fork bounced off his teeth; he bit down, and slowly drew the fork out. He began to chew, unaware that he had nothing in his mouth, and then swallowed. The basic function of feeding himself was there, but something was missing. This was nothing short of pure torture. My father was a rock star, and superhuman in my eyes and he didn't even know he was chewing air.

My stomach turned. I looked at my mother, and my eyes began to fill with tears. Quickly excusing myself from the table, I ran to my room and burst into tears. I didn't want my dad to see my pain. I didn't want him to know that watching the man I loved and looked up to was deteriorating before my eyes and it was ripping my heart in two. I had to be strong for my mother. I knew she saw the pain this was causing me. I couldn't let my tears weaken the strength she had or would need to make it through what was to come. I had a new role. I would have to become the man of the house. I had to dig my feet into my foundation and stay strong. How quickly things shift. All of this was simply too much to handle—the weight of the entire universe was on my shoulders. I needed to shift too. I realized Milan would always be there, but my father may not be. Without a question or a single second thought, I decided that my career was going to be put on hold.

The phone ringing obsessively woke me the next morning. On the other end was Clelia, the booker for the agency in Milan. I had already missed seven calls from her. I took a deep breath and reluctantly said, "Hello." I knew why she was calling. I had sent her an email the night before explaining I was not coming. My father was ill and much worse than I expected.

I had already explained to her in a previous conversation that my dad was sick. This wasn't fresh news to her. The words she spoke still haunt me to this day.

"Well," she began, "You already knew that this day might come. You made a commitment to the agency and clients over here. We have worked tirelessly to book these jobs for you. People die. Accept it. Move on. I expect you on the plane."

I was speechless.

The words burned.

I collected myself and simply said, "I am very sorry for you. I'm sorry you don't feel the way I feel about family." Without leaving a breath for a response, I finished with, "I'm going to be with my dad now."

I hung up and dropped the phone. I knew I would never speak to that woman again, but I would have to explain myself to Tom at Wilhelmina. I was a bit scared of his reaction. He had worked hard at growing my career. I explained the situation. I remember his words vividly.

"I'm seriously so mad at you right now."

I braced myself for what would follow. This decision could cost me my contract with the largest agency in New York.

"I am so upset because you actually think I care what she thinks. I am going to be even more upset if you give one more second of thought to her. Take care of your dad and your family. Don't you worry, I will take care of her."

His words were the reassurance and confidence I needed to know I had made the right decision. I now had to tell my dad.

The mornings were always his best time of the day. By nightfall, he was sluggish and far less responsive.

"I decided I am not going to Milan," I said.

He asked me to reconsider my choice and to go. He knew Milan was a huge stepping stone for my career. He didn't want to be the reason I didn't make it further in this business. That was the man my father was. He loved my brother and me endlessly. He wasn't thinking about himself, he was thinking about me. All I could do was think about him. I refused to listen. There would be no negotiations. My mind was made up. I told him I was staying where I was until he got better. I said those words even though I had a feeling he didn't have long. His skin was already yellowing. He was in and out of conscious thought. I called Caleb and told him he needed to come home. Dad was worse than anyone had led on. I needed him here too.

I didn't care what anyone thought; I was where I was supposed to be. The next few days were some of the worst for my dad. I called a friend, Suzanne, who was a massage therapist and asked her to come by and help him relieve the tension and toxins building in his body. He had started building up fluid throughout his body too. I wanted to ease his pain. He rejected the idea at first, but when Suzanne arrived, he obliged. For two hours she worked on him, moving the fluid around and helping him process the buildup. When the sunroom doors opened, my father smiled and said, "I feel better than I have in ten years." I asked what I owed her, but she wouldn't take a dime. Smiling, she said, "I'm glad I could buy you a little more time." My heart was full.

Sunday came, and I was headed to church. As I was saying my goodbyes, my dad said he wanted to talk to the pastor. Pastor Jeff was a compassionate man. He knew my father's health was failing and he agreed to come and speak with my dad. He told me he could come that day, but with it being Sunday the visit would be short and somewhat crazy. He asked if he could come the next day and spend as much time as my father wanted. I understood his reasoning and reluctantly agreed to Monday. I wasn't sure if my father would even make it through the night, let alone be coherent enough to meet with the good pastor.

When I walked through the front door, my dad called from the sunroom, "Hey buddy."

He anticipated Jeff was following close behind me. When my mom saw that I was alone her eyes fell. My father wasn't speaking much by now, and this would be a major disappointment. I told my dad Pastor Jeff would come the next day. His eyes fell too. Caleb arrived that evening.

Monday came, and mom spent a good deal of time making a hearty lunch for four grown men and herself. Knowing Jeff was coming must have given my dad new hope. You could see the familiar sparkle we were all used to. He didn't look like a sick man. There was hope, a renewed sense of energy. He was wide awake and aware in a way I hadn't seen since I arrived.

When Pastor Jeff arrived, my dad's speech was clear. He was with it. I remember thinking to myself, Jeff isn't going to believe my father is as sick as I said when I asked him to come for a visit.

In the pause of lightheartedness, Jeff asked an important question.

"Where are you at with God?" he asked.

Caleb and I got up and started to leave the sunroom. Shocked by our quick exit, he looked at us both and said, "What did I say?" We smiled and closed the doors. For an hour they spoke in confidence. The French doors opened, and they both entered the kitchen. We sat down to eat lunch and about ten minutes later, my dad, still wide awake and full of ambition, said I need to tell you something. He paused, not because of his illness, but because his emotions were running high. Slowly, I witnessed something I hadn't seen since my grandmother's funeral. His eyes slowly began to fill with water. He started to cry, looked directly at me and said, "I want you to know that I just accepted Christ with Jeff, in the sunroom. You don't have to worry, because you will see me again in heaven one day."

I leaped from my chair. My dad stayed in his seat. I wrapped my arms around his neck from behind and kissed his cheek. Together we wept.

"Thank you," I said.

I told him how much I loved him. I had peace now. That was the burden, the turning in my stomach that made me run from the table nights before. I didn't know if I would see my father in heaven. The thought of this uncertainty kept me awake at night. But now, I knew he knew God and he now held a key to heaven's gate.

My tears were dry until much later. My dad leaned on God in those next coming days, as did everyone else.

Tools in the Toolbox
Tool #8: Knowing Your Place

The phrase "knowing your place" often has a negative connotation. Normally when someone tells you to "know your place" they are referring to the fact they feel you are stepping out of bounds whether with your words or actions in a particular situation. It's important in life to know our boundaries and whether those lines should be crossed.

There is another side to "knowing your place," and it's one that I would like you to see in a positive light.

Think of it like this: We all play different roles in our families, friend groups, jobs, churches—you name it—we take on different responsibilities within our different places in our lives. Realistically evaluate your place in this world. Who are you? Are you a son, husband, father? Daughter, wife, mother? Boss or employee? You understand. Who are you? Where is your place? Do you know and understand your role?

For instance, when my parents needed me the most, I could have been selfish. I could have weighed the options before me and decided my career was more important than staying to help my mother and father during the difficult days ahead. I could have fooled myself into thinking that my father's condition was temporary. I could have carried on, left them to deal with the burden of my father's failing health, but instead I knew my place. I knew I was needed at home. This was my place. I chose to put my career on hold and then placed myself in their shoes—mainly my

111

mother's—and rolled up my sleeves. If a moment calls for it, you have to take the lead.

Have you taken the lead? Are there places in your life that your place is being ignored?

There is always another side to every situation. If my mother refused my help, I would have known to reevaluate the situation and respectfully remain in my place as their son instead of the shifting role of man of the house.

Do you recall in Chapter 1 how I spoke about the fact that I love sharing my faith with anyone who has a listening ear? This is another example of knowing your place. I am always on fire to share the word, but I also know my place. If the message is not welcomed, I choose to show my faith instead of pushing it. Remember what we talked about in planting the seed? Sometimes people need to see something grow. Know your place.

Knowing your place can be a tricky line to walk, but it's a necessary one to address.

Think about this in your life. Are there other people's shoes you can fill? Are there situations that beg you to put your own needs on hold and help someone else? Do you see your place? Do you know where it is?

The reason the phrase "knowing your place" gets a bad rap is due to incidences of speaking before we think. I want to venture to say that every living soul has faced this situation a time or two in their life—that moment when you speak without thinking—where words tumble from your mouth that can never be taken away. Those moments are hard. They're hard not only for the person receiving it, but for the person saying the words too. Before speaking think: Is this a time where I step forward and say something or is this a time where I step back, mind my place, and say nothing at all. Sometimes silence really is golden.

Think of the booking agent's words about my father. They were crude, lacking in compassion, nasty daggers that showed nothing but disrespect for another living soul and me. I was amazed by her words, stunned really. But, I cannot say there haven't been times that I've been the agent to someone's upset.

When emotions are involved, and the stakes are running high, words can pack a more powerful punch than we intend. This is why I say, know your place. If we can understand that not every situation needs a response, we can better understand ourselves and our places in life.

Good or bad, we must know our places. You now have tool #8, Knowing Your Place. It's ready to use to its fullest. Toss it in your toolbox and come along.

Photo Chapter

Welcome to a glimpse into some of my most cherished memories—spanning from my childhood to now. I hope this gives you insight into some of the stories you have and will be reading throughout this book. This chapter was a labor of love. I wanted to make sure I gave credit to those who are so very important to me, and still, I know I am missing so many.

As I was looking through photos, I noticed there was a great difference in the number of photos I have taken during the last ten years of my life. I can only attribute the lack of captured memories to the ease of cell phones and our access to digital capabilities. After searching for these beautiful moments that I knew I wanted to share with you, I grew upset to see how few moments were actually captured with a still frame. If there is one piece of advice you glean from my life story, up until this point, I hope it is that you will take every opportunity to capture the memories you are making today and every day after that. You will thank yourself when years later you are able to match your memory to a captured moment. So please, enjoy this short journey through my life. I do hope you enjoy it.

◀ Squint and Cheese was the cool thing to do back then. My little brother, Caleb on the left. Yours truly is on the right.

▲ Me and some of my best friends from middle school. Teron (left), Dwayne (front), me, and DaNeil (right).

◀ Catching some rays and enjoying the sun with my Dad and Caleb. Clearly, I was big into weightlifting— NOT!

▲ White Carnation Formal for Delta Chi. Hilton Head Island, S.C. 1995. Brothers that were also graduates of Piedmont High School where I attended.

▲ All degreed up! Ready to take on the world. Appalachian State University Class of 1999. From the left, sister-in-law Dora, Caleb, Mom, me, and Dad.

▲ Welcome to the days before digital photography. Yes, we actually had to print photos to see them first. This is a contact sheet that we used to pick the images for our composite cards and portfolios. We even took pictures with a Polaroid camera before the shoot began. No digital photos means no immediate results.

◄ Somebody found the weights and learned how to use them. This is when I was doing fitness modeling and was a personal trainer. I learned to respect the temple that God gifted me.

◀ This is me being me—acting goofy; having fun. Fred Egan Photography.

▲ Real men wear scarves. Photo by Fred Egan

▲ "You know, just posing up in the attic." Jeff Holt

◀ Sean Martin and me in the Big Apple again after our plans were changed by September 11, 2001. Represented by Wilhelmina Modeling Agency.

▲ Me, TEK, Sean Martin and Dennis O'Neal.

On the end of the runway having fun. ▼

▲ Having fun opening a new store.

A man, his dog, and a good cup of coffee.
Photo by Jeff Holt

My Father, My Hero

▲ The last time I felt my father's hand upon my shoulder praising my abilities as I showed him the mural. Yes, that little white square on the picture to the right is an outlet.

◀ "Now you see where I got it."

▲ Visiting my dad at Christmas. My mom and I always put a tree up for him. My favorite ornament is one of my signed carpenter pencils from the show.

◀ "Thanks for the good genes. Love and miss you."

My most cherished award and it wasn't
even given to me. The Dennis Russell
Diligence Award. Saying I'm proud is an
understatement.

◀ The Big Deal stage being used to serve God!
▼

Bless & Be Blessed. Hudson helping make a sizzle reel for a show I wrote. ▼

▲ My LifeGroup road trip to see Josh Wilson in concert. From the back left, Stevie, right back, Hudson, Front seat, Chris rocking the dreads, and of course me in the driver seat.

A Role Model

▲   My LifeGroup being the church. We filled Easter baskets to give to young children.

◄   Alex, Chris and me at Hebron Rock Falls in Boone, North Carolina. We took a trip for Alex to see Appalachian State. He now attends my Alma mater.

Had to play to the camera, right? Alex and I having a blast at the falls.
▶

▲ Here is my kitchen before I remodeled the space.

▲ My kitchen after a remodel. I repurposed the same cabinets by sanding, trimming, and painting them.

▲ Before picture. My hall bath with silver and red velvet wallpaper. The tile was pink!

▲ I swear this is the same bath now with travertine. Skillz Son!

A Carpenter's Hands

▲ "Maverick Rock Taco" bar before remodel.

▲ "Maverick Rock Taco" bar after remodel. I promise it's the same bar.

▲ Nothing screams "Murica" like a 9' x 6' American beer can flag. "Ale's University."

▲ "Char Bar 7" custom lit sign. It's made from wood and metal. Yeah, I made that!

◀ Kowabunga 20'x10' wave I painted for a restaurant.

American Flag 29'x 11' distressed wood. ▶

It's a good thing I'm not afraid of heights! Art knows no limits.

A Carpenter's Hands

◄ Laying out a new design. Before ...

▲ After...

I designed the outside of this cigar humidor. The wall is covered in the tops of all the cigars inside the humidor. The space was featured in a popular Charlotte magazine. ▼

Custom wine rack I built for a restaurant. ▼

Reclaimed wood walls are the current trend. This was a labor of intense love.

▲ Who doesn't love a custom treehouse? This is a paradise for kids!

▲ The first thing I ever Brazed (welded) with my good friend, Michael Haun. The cross is a keychain that I still use everyday.

◄ Even our four-legged friends need a paradise of their own. This is my dog, "Revel," short for Revelation. I got him after my father passed. I turned this closet into his space.

▲ Custom built sign for "Maverick Rock Taco" bar.

My first episode on Trading Spaces. The homeowners opened the back of the truck to see Designer Frank Bielec and I ready to trade spaces!

◀ Getting ready to be crowned the Soap Box Champion on Trading Spaces. I built the car and Frank painted it. I still have it.

These guys helped make television magic happen. Stew and Chris were the background carpenters that helped pull everything together. It was a pleasure to work with them. ▶

◀ Merry Christmas from Trading Spaces. I'm an Elf, not Peter Pan.

The ladies of Savannah State University. Trading Spaces went back to school to fix up a room. ▶

◀ One of the many talented designers that graced the Trading Spaces team.

The most beautiful, amazing, caring, loving mom and woman in the entire world. What? My book! My rules! She wins #1 mom!

Mrs. Martha Russell, my mom. ▶

Ziplining in Las Vegas, NV ▶

◀ We love to be creative together too.

Mom visiting me on the set of Trading Spaces. ▶

A Glimpse of My Family

▲ My niece, Briana born in 2004.

▲ My nephew, John Michael born in 2010.

▲ My niece, Ava born in 2006.

▲ Briana and Ava may have the modeling gene!

A Glimpse of My Family

Helping to create the perfect flower garden for my niece, Ava's bedroom. ▶

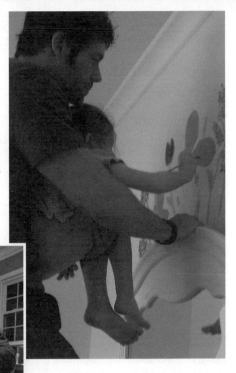

Creating canvases for John Michael's nursery before he was born.

My nieces and nephew are growing up fast.

Our last family vacation together. My dad,
mom, me, sister-in-law Dora, and Caleb.

◀ Friends in Charlotte, North Carolina.

Sorry for giving you your first brain freeze, Ethan.
▼

▲ Church tailgate party to watch the Panthers with my friend Chris and his two sons, Ethan and Eli.
▶

Taking a break in the middle of Time Square with my friend, Jodi. ▶

Protecting the ladies! Happy Halloween and Happy Birthday to me. ▼

My good friend Jason's wedding weekend. Jason, me and Travis Van Winkle. ▶

Hanging out with some of the younger brothers of Delta Chi. ▼

Peanut Butter & Jelly
Lauren Makk and Me

Trading Spaces
days. Striking a pose
before dinner. ▶

▲ At Lauren's store, PAD in Hawaii. I
helped teach a D-I-Y bench making class.

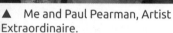

▲   Me and Paul Pearman, Artist Extraordinaire.

◀   Paul's superb handy work. He crafted this belt buckle for my tool belt.

Hanging out with my good friend..." please just change the change the acronym to "LYLAB"   ▼

04/30/2

▲   Charity event for the Sisken School. Once this little casanova, Jonathan blew a kiss to the crowd, I had no chance. He completely melted everyone's hearts.

◀ My little buddy, Revel.

My 79' Jeep CJ7 from when I was 16. She is still ticking and costing me money today! ▼

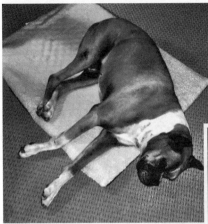

▲ One of my Delta Chi little brothers, Josh, and me hanging out at a Halloween party.

Building alumni / undergraduate relations with younger Delta Chi members at UNCC. ▶

A Glimpse Inside My Life
A collection of great memories

◀ Muhsin "Moose" Muhammad #87. Former Carolina Panther and NFL Pro Football Player. Amazing football player, but even bigger heart for others and his community.

▲ The gang all watching Super Bowl 50! Can you tell who we were rooting for? Go Panthers! Keep Pounding!

◀ Enough said! Help resurrect the front porch community from the back desk society we've become by visiting www.fixitforward.com

Chapter 10
Bless and Be Blessed
"The King will reply, 'Truly I tell you, whatever you did for one of the least of these brothers and sisters of mine, you did for me.'"
Matthew 25:40

There is no such thing as luck or happenstance. As I said before, everything happens in God's perfect timing. I would go a bit further saying I don't believe in coincidence either. Things happened according to the overall plan, whether we know why things are happening that way or not, we each have a course. God's hands were certainly in my father's final days.

My dad was losing more capacities with each day that passed, both mentally and physically. While I knew the man I loved and treasured as my father was still inside the body being overtaken by an unforgiving disease, the glow he had about himself was starting to dim. I was rightfully worried.

I asked his nurse the question that had been weighing heavily on my mind: how much longer? With a gentle ease and tone, she delivered the bad news. His time was coming. God would soon be calling him home, and she wasn't altogether sure that his time wouldn't come within the next twenty-four hours.

She had been present for many deaths. She knew the signs. She had a sound intuition about these sorts of things. My father's nails were turning blue. Oxygen wasn't being delivered to his entire system. His breath was labored. He was jaundiced. His kidneys and liver were failing. In fact, his whole system was ready to wave the white flag. He had fought hard. I was so proud of his grace; never complaining, he just faced what came. Still, my heart was breaking.

Death is ugly she said. It wasn't like the movies where they closed their eyes and slipped away. Things happen to the shell left behind.

It was time to make some tough decisions. Dad was still set up in the sunroom. His view of the outside was priceless. If he couldn't be outdoors, he could at the very least enjoy them. The nurse reminded me that this beautiful spot in my parents' house had seen enough sadness. If my father passed in this room, she was worried my mother would not do well, that the memory would stay with her forever. In her mind, it would be one thing for my mother to lose the love of her life, the man she had spent more than thirty years with, but it would be another to do so in the home they had built and shared together. The rush of people that would have to be called after he drew his last breath could traumatize my mother. Her thoughts were, dad's time was coming and it was now time to consider the after-effects. Simply put, we needed a plan B.

Dad hated hospitals. I knew the last thing he wanted was to pass in a place he despised. He had spent enough time shuffling from doctor's appointment to doctor's appointment, in and out of those heavy rolling doors—that was the very last place he would want to eternally close his eyes. I wanted to respect those wishes, but I also needed to protect my mother. That is what a son does when life gets turned upside down. They protect everyone they love. I was simply trying to do my best.

I asked about hospice care. The nurse warned me she didn't think it was possible. There was rarely a time when a spot was available, plus there was a waiting list to get in. People die every day, but this time, it was my person. I wanted and needed a place for my father. I didn't much care if there was a list or not. The nurse called, tried her best, but there was nothing available. We would have to go with plan C.

God's miracles often start many days, months, and even years before they fully show themselves. In this case, our miracle began roughly three years before.

My mom is the charitable type. A woman who sees a need and fills it. It's one of the parts I adore about her. My mother caught wind of an event being hosted at the country club where she and my dad were members. They were raising money to support the local hospice care center.

She stepped forward to help after seeing the items that had been donated in the silent auction up to that point were small. Mom knew she could improve their chances if she stepped forward to help their cause. She put her thinking cap on, made some calls, and gathered larger donations. She had no invested interest in the center; it was just something fun for her to do. In the end, Martha Russell helped to turn that previously small silent auction into a night to be forever remembered and a financial success.

The director thanked her and asked for her assistance in the future, but honestly, this wasn't something my mom wanted to do in the long term. It was something she wanted to do in the now. Mom had filled the present need. She was happy with that. They parted ways, leaving behind God's little connection.

Back to my father; the morning of October 29, 2002, there was no room at the hospice care center. Dad was growing worse with each hour. Something had to be done and it needed to be done soon. Around noon, I finally made the decision I was struggling with; he needed to be moved to the hospital. It needed to happen now, or I was afraid it would be too late.

Dad's nurse stepped aside to answer a phone call, but when she came back, her face was lit with joy. She had amazing news. A miraculous opening had just become available at the hospice care center. She didn't know how it happened; this was rare, to say the least, but there was one room. If we wanted it, it was ours, and dad would be admitted immediately. Of course, she knew the answer. Talk about a timely answer to a prayer. The transport team and ambulance were set up, as were the details. Now, the only thing we *all* had to do was wait until they arrived.

The doorbell rang about three hours later. Dad had held on; we all had. As the bell called out again, my mom had no idea the shock that was waiting for her on the other side of the door.

Standing on the stoop was the director of the hospice care center that my mom met at the silent auction three years before. The two women, the director, and my mom looked at one another, shed a tear, embraced in a hug, and realized that a full-circle moment was happening before our very eyes. My mother had blessed the facility years before; now they were about to be our blessing.

The weather outside matched our moods. It was cold, rainy, and the outside air felt as heavy and gloomy as the inside of my chest. My father loved fall. He loved flannel shirts and hot coffee. He loved the trees changing under a brilliant sun. This day would not be that day.

By late afternoon, my father was settled. His side of the family began to arrive.

He was unable to talk, but he held my hand. I want to think he squeezed it a few times, but he wasn't able to move much by now. Yet, I know I felt his hand move in mine. We talked to him. Spent time. We all said our good-byes. Still, he continued to hold on.

The nurse told me what his final breath would look and sound like. She said he would take one last deep breath, and when he let it go, his soul would slip away on the breeze of that exhale. I watched. I waited. But still, he continued to breathe slow and shallow breaths. It's hard to watch someone's final hours, waiting for them to give in, succumb to God's call. But still, I waited.

The hours were drawing us closer to Halloween, my birthday. I wasn't trying to be selfish, I truly wasn't, but internally, I didn't want my father to pass on my birthday. I didn't want that memory connected to that day when it came to celebrating another year of life when it was my father's last.

Afternoon turned to evening, and he was barely hanging on, but he was there. I continued to rack my brain. What was he *holding* on for? What did he need? And then it hit me. This was about my mother.

I sat beside him and slid my hand into his. Leaning in so close my lips were nearly touching his ear, I whispered, in a hush, these words: "If you are worried about mom, please, don't be. I promise I will take care of her and all of her needs. She is safe with me. You can let go."

That was it. Those were the words that had been keeping his soul tied to this earthly plane. With a slight squeeze of my hand, my father's broad and powerful chest filled one last time. He drew in as much oxygen as his body could hold and as he exhaled this breath of life his soul slipped away. I had lost my father at the tender age of twenty-six, just two days shy of my twenty-seventh birthday.

There are two ways to death. One is sudden and comes without the ability to say goodbye. While this is heartbreaking, there is a positive. The person did not suffer, but the negative is those left behind unexpectedly lose someone they did not get to say their last goodbyes to.

The other way to death is when someone slowly passes away. The negative here is that oftentimes there is suffering and pain. The positive is loved ones get the opportunity to say goodbye and let the person know how much they care. I have to say I hated to see my father drift away, yet, I'm so thankful I was able to tell him how special he was to me—how I was able to say that I will always cherish the life and gifts he gave to me. God's perfect timing had come.

His funeral was devastating and perfect all at the same time. Devastating because I lost my hero, my friend, my amazing father. But perfect in the way that the weather he so greatly loved shined in all its glory. The sun was bright and high in the sky. The fall breeze blew. I like to think of my father looking down that day, and having a hand in orchestrating the weather.

I once heard someone describe death as God's way of reaching into His garden and picking the most beautiful roses for heaven's bouquet. That just like we do here on earth when picking flowers for our centerpieces, we always pluck the most beautiful flowers from the stem giving it life. God does the same, but with one rewarding difference. He picks the most beautiful flowers for heaven and in this sense plucks us from our stem here on earth but gives us a life to live eternally in heaven. I know that my dad added unequaled beauty to God's perfect garden. Isn't it beautiful to think, the flower wilts and fades away here on earth, but our soul shines and dances in His presence in heaven when we are picked? It's stunning.

I miss my father. While I know anyone can imagine the way losing a parent can feel, until you have experienced the actual loss, words cannot begin to touch the deepness of those emotions. I miss my father's laughter, his smile, the sound advice, and firm hand patting me upon the shoulders with reassurance when I need it most. But in the end, I know God's plan is always moving me forward. I just didn't know how true those words actually were until a short time later.

Tools in the Toolbox
Tool #9: Diligence
"Therefore, brothers, be all the more diligent to make your calling and election sure, for if you practice these qualities you will never fall."
2 Peter 1:10

Diligence: the characteristic of being careful and persistent in your effort and in the work you are called to do. That is a powerful statement. The action of being diligent is even more powerful when used in life.

This tool is especially dear to my heart because it's the tool my father strived to model in his own life. His actions were some of the greatest lessons for my brother and me. He taught us how to be successful men because he used diligence in every single thing he did. After my dad passed, his company, Clarke Industries, asked our family if we could attend that year's company banquet. They wanted to honor his life for all he had done within their workplace. That night was so much more than that, however. My mom, Caleb, and I were called to the stage. As photos of my father played on the screen behind us, his accomplishments were read, and in the end, we were presented with an award titled the Dennis Russell Diligence Award. It is the highest honor a salesman within the company could ever receive. Each year a new recipient receives this award that has been dedicated in my father's name. It's a true testament to the character my father showed not only in his work environment but also in his home.

I'd never felt so much gratification than I had that night. It made me realize the importance of what diligence is. Diligence is spoken about repeatedly in the Bible. God asks us to be diligent in our passion for him, in spreading his word, and living a life in his image. If you apply diligence to the practice of all the other tools, then you will be pleasing in the eyes of the Lord because you are acting in a way that is persistent in following Him.

Diligence is one of the highest honors to possess in your character. There are several ways to foster this tool if it is something you are still starving to master.

Practice these tips: Remove distractions like social media, television, and outside sources that pull you away from your destination or goal.

Make a list that helps you use your time efficiently.

Devote yourself to your plan, your call, and God's word.

Be realistic about your goals and plans. Being realistic will help you be diligent in your pursuits.

Lastly, always remember the value of the work you are doing. Value adds meaning and helps push us further.

This essential tool is God's goal for us. The lessons my father taught me are honestly the tool I use the most in my everyday life. I make it a point not to give in even if the road gets rocky and tough. I never give up. I use challenges to push me to work harder. If I put my mind to a task, I diligently pursue the goal with the mindset that I'm serving a higher purpose.

Think of the diligence my father showed in his last days. He wouldn't give in or up until he knew the woman he loved so dearly, my mom, was taken care of. Unable to speak, he held on, taking shallow breath after shallow breath, until I finally whispered the words he needed to hear.

He had diligently been the husband who took the oath of marriage, the promises he made my mother, and to God so seriously he practiced this tool up until his final moments here on earth.

Be diligent. Command diligence. Craft and use this tool in everything you do. Are there places in your life where diligence is lacking? Are you diligent in your faith? Are you diligent in following the path you are called to follow and create? Is there anything on the list above that you can improve upon to help you construct an award-winning life?

You now have tool #9, Diligence. If you are ready to be faithfully diligent, toss this tool in your toolbox and come along.

Chapter 11
A Carpenter's Tools

The day my father passed, things changed as they tend to do. A new season started in my life whether I was ready or not. As I said in the very beginning of this book, a carpenter is only as good as the tools in his toolbox. My father's workshop was overflowing with an array of instruments and apparatuses, some I had never noticed before. With his tools now in my possession, I realized that my long-held belief of carpenters actually worked the opposite way.

Tools are only as good as the carpenter that knows how to use them. I had a lot to learn, but first, things would have to settle into a new routine.

I'll proudly admit this rugged carpenter that can fix anything that challenges him, highly independent, self-proclaimed tough guy is also a huge momma's boy—it's actually something I take pride in—with our relationship being as close as it is, there was no way I was going let her be alone at this time in her life. Caleb and my sister-in-law, Dora had to return home to Charlotte. I could work with my agency in Atlanta for the time being and be home where she needed me. It was the perfect plan, and to tell you the truth as much as I felt she needed me, I needed my mom too.

The house was quiet. Things were left undone, and as I had promised my father I would, I was going to take care of my mom. My place in New York was sublet until the first of December being that I was supposed to be in Milan all this time. Staying put in Atlanta was the obvious choice for many reasons.

My birthday passed, and November arrived. In my mind, my mother would want to downsize in the near future. My parent's house is much too large for just one person and the time would come that she would be alone in the house. I headed to the basement and stood in my father's workshop.

Let me rewind for a moment. After college, I moved back in with my parents. Modeling had me traveling a large majority of the time and it only made logical sense not to waste money on a place I would only stay at a few nights out of each month.

Dad and I had started finishing their basement during this time. The house was a ranch-style with a full basement. My dad had finally gotten his dream home. He left the basement framed out, plumbed, and wired so that he could finish it to his liking. The plan was to divide the space into an entertainment/home theater room, workout space, office, workshop, hunting and fishing room, and then he would have his man cave area. It was everything he could have needed and so much more.

Dad expanded on the lessons he taught me as a teenager and began teaching me the art of hanging sheetrock. It was hard work, but together we created walls that defined the space. While he was away on business, I asked a friend to paint a mural of Augusta National's 11th and 12th green as a gift to him on the back wall of his sports bar. The house was located in a golf community and my dad now loved his time on the golf course. My friend wasn't available at the time and urged me to paint the mural myself. She knew my art skills could handle the challenge, so I gave it a try.

This was the first time I had ever painted a mural, let alone a mural of this size. It was huge—fifteen feet long by eight feet high. I recreated the entire scene by looking at a 5x7 postcard. Little did I know that this project would turn out better than even I expected. I turned over a new leaf and added a new seed of creativity that I would use later in life.

When my father returned to town, I was eighty-five percent done with the project, but the anticipation got the best of me, and I let him see the mural. He was absolutely floored at the sight of it. He couldn't believe I was able to do that in such little time, considering how much detail I had placed in the azaleas and the hues that shaded the shadows from the sun over the sand traps.

Now, back to the days that followed after my father passed, the basement still needed work—lots of work, in fact. If my mom ever wanted to sell the house, the basement needed to be completed to get the maximum amount for resale. The work still left undone was such that I hadn't the slightest clue how to do it on my own. I was up for the challenge, but it also meant I had to expand upon my knowledge. What my father had taught me wasn't enough to finish the downstairs space. Like most homeowners with a problem to address, I headed to the internet and watched dozens of how-to videos.

With what little knowledge I collected on the World Wide Web I taught myself how to wire a home theater system, finish drywall, apply a perfect stain, and tile a floor. I also enlisted the help of dad's brother, my Uncle Leslie. He was a master plumber and skilled craftsman in his own right. I loved working next to my uncle. He taught me a thing or two about plumbing and the correct way to hang crown molding.

For a month, I labored downstairs. I messed up a million times, correction—a million and one times—but when I finished, I had gained skills no one could ever take from me. My father's tools didn't own me; I owned them.

December arrived, and my apartment in New York was open. There is absolutely nothing that can compare to Christmastime in the city. It's truly magical. Mom and I booked a flight and headed to the Big Apple. For fifteen days, we took in the sights and sounds of New York City.

We enjoyed each other's company, and it allowed us not to feel the grief looming over either of us for a moment. When we returned, I stayed in Atlanta through the New Year and decided it was time for me to take a new leap of faith.

At the age of twenty-nine, I felt it was time to give Hollywood a shot. Mom was as settled as she was going to be, so I packed up and headed for the West Coast. Several years before I had been cast to star in a television show that was slated to be a prominent network's answer to *The*

Bachelor's wild success. The details are long and drawn out and, in the end, the show was unable to get off the ground, but one amazing thing did come out of the experience. I met a casting agent who believed in me.

During the time I was headed out to L.A., she was going to be traveling for two months and offered her home in Brentwood, rent-free, to see if I could make a name for myself among the Hollywood elite. With nothing to lose, I jumped at the opportunity.

It just so happened that around the same time, a close friend of mine, Travis Van Winkle, was also headed to L.A. to give fame a shot. He and I met after his mom, who was a nurse, showed me a picture of him at one of my doctor's appointments. I agreed that Travis had the right look to make it in the modeling world and made a call on his behalf. He was doing well for himself, but like me he knew there were more opportunities in California. A couple of weeks into my stay, Travis and I met up. I went on auditions, but nothing was coming together the way I thought it should. I gave it my best effort, but in the end, I decided it was time for me to think about doing something else.

Walking down Hollywood Boulevard, Travis and I were discussing the future. I explained I had been doing some thinking, and it was time for me to reevaluate what I really wanted to accomplish in my life. It was time for me to leave L.A. and go home.

When I say home, I mean home to the place I most considered to be my comfort spot—North Carolina. After traveling for so many years, I realized that this was truly the only place I found myself smiling from ear to ear. The place I didn't wish for something more. North Carolina was home, and I needed to get back to that fundamental part of me.

My brother had called me two weeks before this conversation and offered me an opportunity I couldn't refuse. His father-in-law and brother-in-law lived in a beautiful, well established neighborhood in the heart of North Carolina. Beautiful oak trees line the neighborhood. It's truly a southerner's haven. They had decided to buy it and flip it for resale. My brother mentioned to them that I was interested in buying a home and settling down in hopes of one day getting married and starting a family of my own. They all agreed they would be happy to have me as a neighbor and would look for another investment property. I was still in L.A. and wouldn't make it back in time to purchase the home before it went on the market so I made the suggestion that I would buy it, but if I didn't care for the property they could move forward with flipping it. The plans were all put into action.

With a place to lay my head, I told Travis my decision had been made. I was twenty-nine. Travis was only twenty-one. As he urged me not to give up chasing my dreams, I explained to him that he still had seven years before he reached my age. In Hollywood, the standard is every month four thousand hopefuls drive, fly, or sail into the city with hopes of being the next megastar. At the same time, five thousand take the departing flight out with their dreams in their saddle bags. It takes time to break into television and movies. I knew I didn't have that time.

It was time to see where the next road would lead. Once I returned, I settled into my new home. It needed a ton of work, but with the knowledge I learned in the basement of my parents' house, the mastery over my father's tools, and the ability to figure out whatever skills I was lacking, I went to work. It didn't come with a few hiccups, however. It wasn't long before I realized I had never wanted my father by my side more than I would in the next days and months.

Some have trouble with holidays or their loved ones' birthdays, but for me, those aren't the times that I find myself aching from the loss of my father. I suppose I build myself up in preparation of the special days. I know Christmas will come whether or not my father is there to decorate the big, live tree he so greatly loved, but it's the little moments that grab hold and nearly refuse to let go. What affected me more than anything was when I grabbed for one of my father's tools. It was a give and take.

I would be ripping out the tile, grab for the hammer, and see visions of my father. The man, no matter how knowledgeable he was in his craft, lacked patience. That is actually being incredibly kind. The man was impatient and was quick to frustrate if things didn't come together with ease. We all have our flaws; this was his. His example taught me the number one rule of carpentry: you count on things not working out the way you planned or expected.

I laugh now, but when I was a young teenager, my father and I were working on a cabin. We were standing on an elevated porch. Things were going wrong and in a moment of being hot-headed my dad threw his hammer as hard as he could. It sailed to the ground below and landed in a menagerie of brown wilting leaves and broken twigs. There would be no way we would ever find that hammer again. It clicked, even then, that allowing frustration to take over and not having the patience to regroup only made things worse in the long run. Without the hammer, now what were we going to do?

With each old memory that floated through my head, I learned a new life lesson, such as patience, as I worked to build a place I could call my own. I messed up—I learned from doing things wrong. There was freedom in knowing each new project I tackled taught me something, and that I had the freedom to mess it up and start anew. I cannot tell you how many pieces of wood I cut wrong. It's just part of learning.

I designed and built a built-in bookcase and entertainment center in my living room. By then I had mastered the skill of hiding the nails. It was a big project but after dozens of finishing nails, the piece was a showstopper. It was quite the undertaking and one I was proud I had accomplished.

Little did I know, I should have glued the wood together before I added the nails. I never glued anything together. The glue seemed so unnecessary. That is what nails were for, or so I thought. I had it all wrong. Later I

learned that the glue was the key to everything. The nails
weren't there to hold the piece together. The nails were
there to allow the glue to set and make the piece stronger.

As I carried on the renovations to the home, I honed
my craft and educated myself in a way that most do not
take the time to do, until one day the truest test came.

I was walking out and noticed a puddle of water on the
floor in the garage. I looked up and realized my master
shower was directly above where the water had pooled. It
hit me, the shower pan had to be leaking. I had plans to
redo the shower, expand, and retile it at some point, but it
certainly wasn't on the immediate needs list. I tore the
shower out, took it down to the studs and rotten wood floor.
The shower pan had seen better days and definitely needed
replacing. In expanding the shower base, I had to relocate
the drain. It seemed easy enough until I realized the three-
inch cast iron pipe from sometime in the 1960s wasn't
going to be as easy to reposition as I had presumed. I
needed expert advice. I headed to a local plumbing supply
warehouse and explained the situation. Overall, the plan
was flawed. I would have to carefully remove the furring
strip, an older style of packing, and carefully secure the
connection of the pipes to keep water from leaking. The
problem was the pipe could easily crack or loosen.

The entire job was a risk.

For two hours, I worked restlessly. I tried my best to
channel the lessons I learned about having patience from
my father, but I was slowly teetering on the threshold of
utter frustration. I was in over my head. In my head, I kept

asking myself, what was I thinking. Self-doubt had started to set in. I should never have bought a house and thought I could do all of this alone. I needed my dad. I knew he could fix anything, and he would have been able to help. I never had wanted to pick up the phone and call him for advice more than I did right then.

I positioned myself in the corner where a shower pan used to exist with very little room to spare or I would fall through the opening in the floor. I sat there looking at the ceiling.

"Why?" I called out.

Why was this happening to me?

"Dad," I pleaded. "I can't tell you how bad I need your advice and help right now."

As I was lifting my hands upward and out away from me in frustration and disappointment, I sort of caught my balance by placing my hand on the two-by-four near the shower water lines that were exposed. When I did, I grazed the hot water pipe that supplied the water to the nozzle. A single drop of water fell on my hand. That was suspicious. I had turned off the water and there should have been no way that anything was able to pass through the line.

Investigating further, I noticed two feet up from the shower floor there was a ninety-degree elbow that was covered in a bright green buildup. Calcium had hardened around the elbow where water was leaking in the hot water supply line. I knew this situation could occur if the soldering copper does not fully seal, but by the looks of things, there was no way to determine how long the leak had been occurring. It appeared that it had been happening for years.

I reached up, making sure I was correct, and definitely felt water. Logically speaking, it made sense that the area with the most decayed area in the wooden floor under the shower pan must have been the source of the leak. But then I noticed that even the two-by-four above the floor was rotting only up to the height of where the elbow joint was. It hit me. That is where the leak was coming from; it wasn't the shower pan after all.

If it hadn't been for that moment of wishing for my father's help, I wouldn't have discovered the real issue in the shower. I would have put in a new shower pan, retiled it, and thought all is well—problem solved.

I still like to think it was my dad who answered my pleas, once again offering guidance when I needed him the most. With a renewed sense of faith in my abilities, I knew there was another way to fix the pipe. Although the experts told me it would be impossible to cut through the three-inch cast iron pipe, I grabbed my dad's tiger saw and a metal blade. I cut through that so-called impenetrable pipe in less than a minute. I couldn't believe how fast I cut through it, not to mention the fact that I had wasted three hours of time trying to disconnect the pipe when all I had to do was cut it. I quickly realized that with an ounce of patience, and doing some things wrong the first time allowed me to discover the true root of the problem.

So, the truth is now out. I just revealed the big secret to all my carpentry magic tricks.

People always see the things I have built and ask how I know how to build the things I do. The answer is simple. It's because I've already done it five ways wrong. Luckily, they only see the result of patience and practice. Somewhere in all that remodeling, I became a carpenter and the master of my toolbox.

Tools in the Toolbox
Tool #10: Patience
"Patience is not passive; on the contrary, it is active; it is concentrated strength."
Edward Bulwer-Lytton

How many times have you heard the saying "Patience is a virtue?" I know I've heard this old German Proverb countless times. But have you honestly sat down and thought about what those words mean? Let's first define the meaning of the word virtue.

A virtue, simply put, is being of moral excellence. It's a good or admirable quality. Patience in the most basic definition means being even-tempered or of steady perseverance. If you combine the two definitions, the saying would mean: being even-tempered is to be of moral excellence.

Think about that! Those are big shoes to fill in every single facet of life. Is it possible to be even-tempered at every turn? For those who answer yes, I would ask is that something that is learned or is it built into your disposition.

From my point of view, patience either comes naturally or it must be cultivated and nurtured over time. In some instances, patience isn't an art that is learned at all. I mentioned I was lucky to come to understand what losing your patience looked like at an early age. Learning by example doesn't always mean the example is the correct one shown. My father's inability to be patient when working on a project taught me I could control myself from

168

letting things bother me and accept that things may not go right the first time.

When we lose the ability to self-calm, we put ourselves in a dangerous state. What happens in rush hour traffic? Someone is impatient, cuts another person off, road rage ensues, and oftentimes an accident occurs.

If the guilty party or parties took a deep breath and realized those extra seconds actually cost far less than a ticket or damage to their car, in the end, they could have saved themselves an awfully big headache. Decisions made in haste often cause the situation to be worse.

I'll come clean. I've been known to be impatient at times. I find myself getting upset when the clock strikes close to a deadline. Or when the project fell only on my shoulders when ten people were all tasked to collaborate on the same item. But what I've learned is to slow down, take a deep breath, count to ten, and reevaluate the situation. The reason patience is a virtue is because of the ability to control yourself in a stressful situation.

If you operate as my father did, try a few of these tips to instill patience:

Pinpoint your triggers. Do you become more impatient if you are stressed or have anxiety?

Reduce your overall stress.

Take one day where your focus and goal for the entire day is to make a concerted effort to be patient in every situation you encounter.

Pace yourself. If you have a tendency to procrastinate, you are causing yourself undue stress by pressuring yourself to push to meet an unrealistic deadline. This behavior develops a breeding ground for impatience.

Ask yourself if the situation will be helped or harmed by your lack of patience.

Practice delayed gratification. We live in a world of "nows!" If you want another dessert or a third pair of running shoes, make yourself wait. See if the feelings pass. This simple skill builds patience.

Practice patience by thinking before you speak.

Add in a physical activity that requires focus and patience to see a result.

Any of these items can help you channel your energy in a positive way and help your virtue grow. God wants us to show peace and patience both for our fellow man and for ourselves.

I know all too well the countless times I have had to practice patience while the events happening before me opened bigger doors and greater blessings. Think about the shower in my home. I had to slow down, settle into peace, and regroup because in the end that was the only way I would have found the leak. That patience leads to me mastering my tools, both physically and emotionally.

Lastly, I will leave you with one of my personal quotes: "Take it easy. Take it slow, but always stay ahead." To fulfill this quote requires a mindset rooted in the foundation of patience.

Take it easy by not causing undue stress; plan ahead. Take it slow, simply do not rush. Savor the moments and appreciate your surroundings and journey. Most importantly, find balance by always staying ahead. When you are able to always be ahead while learning to plan ahead, you allow for patience, you remove potential anxiety and frustration, and you truly master the active ability to concentrate your strengths in everything you do.

This tool requires you to use it to fully acquire it. Tool #10, Patience, is ready for your mastery. Toss it in your toolbox and come along.

Chapter 12
Non-Negotiable: I Surrender
"The reason why many are still troubled, still seeking, still making little forward progress is because they haven't yet come to the end of themselves. We're still trying to give orders, and interfering with God's work within us."
A.W. Tozer

If you stand your ground, you are blessed forward. Let me explain. I hadn't lived in North Carolina for more than four years when I returned and purchased my home. A fraternity brother that attended the Bible studies in college shared my affinity for the Tar Heels—particularly basketball. Knowing I had settled in, he knew I would soon be searching for a new church home.

He invited me to church, enticing me with the fact that the head pastor was David Chadwick, a former Tar Heel basketball all-star. I took the bait, and boy am I glad I did. I later came to realize that had I not stepped up as Chaplain all those years before, what was waiting for me behind these church doors wouldn't have been recommended or received.

I want to explain up front that I personally believe that there are two important steps to becoming a Christian. The first is through acceptance of Christ as your Savior, and the second is you must surrender to Christ. There is a difference. Both can happen at the same time, but they can also happen independently of each other. For me, they

172

didn't happen at the same time. I accepted Christ at seventeen. The first time I surrendered happened at age twenty-nine. There was a highly important word in that last sentence—first, the first time I surrendered happened at age twenty-nine. Experiences began to prove that if I wanted to walk on God's faithful path, then I had to surrender to Christ daily. I had to resist the temptation of any and all sin, but even then some of the biggest lessons came from the hardest inner struggles.

The house was coming along great. I was beginning to travel more and more for work. I had built my base of modeling up enough that I was able to live in Charlotte and book jobs to any city that called. It would give me a chance to establish myself in North Carolina again too. Having returned from L.A. I knew I wanted to chase the idea of family, but I still had to pay the bills and the shoestring budget I used to handle the house remodeling.

I hated the idea of the house sitting vacant during my extended stays away. I decided to get a roommate that would help keep the house occupied while I was gone. Plus, with all the hard work I had put into fixing up the place, and so much space between the walls, I felt like I shouldn't have been the only one to enjoy it.

I had fallen into a bad living situation during college. The details are pointless really, but what I knew was that once I found the perfect roommate, I wouldn't ask anyone to commit to a long-term lease, nor would I force their hand into a six-month agreement. I wanted to operate on a gentleman's agreement only. Should they decide to move, I would ask for two months' notice.

That would allow me to find someone else to fill their space, while continuing to have the security of knowing the house was being watched while I was away.

Plus, I would be lying if I didn't say I liked the extra security of knowing the mortgage didn't all fall on my shoulders, even if I could afford it. It also added to my drive to work more. When life is secure and settled, it's then when it seems I work the hardest.

A guy I knew from high school needed a place to live. It seemed like a natural fit and the perfect solution. Everything was going great. My career was heading upward again. I had a roommate onboard, and God had opened my eyes to my new church home at Forest Hill. I began taking roles within the church, leading a Bible study and a LifeGroup. With my heart ignited and life moving at a good clip, I asked my roommate to come along one Sunday morning. He declined the offer. I let it go.

Over the next month, I asked a few more times. Sharing my experiences at Forest Hill, listening to the whisper in my ear that he needed a place to call home, but still with each attempt came the same answer. He had no interest or call to worship with me. Armed with the knowledge that I planted the seed, I finally let the conversation die. He would come when and if he was ready. I knew my place.

Things went on like this for a while. Then one afternoon I got word that my roommate was moving out.

This was the first I had heard of it. The two-month agreement we had standing seemed to be of little concern to him. Worse, I didn't hear the news from my roommate's mouth; it was delivered by a mutual friend. I was angry, to say the least. Immediately grabbing my phone, I sent him a text for him to call me.

I didn't allow myself any space to breathe. My blood was pulsing, my heart was racing, and my tone matched the flurry of activity jittering through my body as the phone rang. The patience I prided myself on was lost. A firm sternness filled my tone when I heard the word "hello."

My southern courtesy was as good as gone too. "I heard you are moving out," I began.

The news was true. A place had opened up. It was cheaper than the rent I charged and he and the other friend had a stronger bond. Overall, this is what was best for everyone, he said. Everyone but me.

"When are you planning on moving?" I asked.

The first of March was his response. It was the day before Valentine's Day. Fifteen measly days was a far cry from the sixty days we had agreed upon when he first moved in. I was shocked and growing more irate with each passing moment.

"As in March of next year, right?" I questioned hotly.

I knew better, but I wanted to hear the words from his mouth and not someone else's. He owed me that. Confirmation came that his exit was two short weeks away. This timeframe was unacceptable and if I had my way this wasn't the way all of this was going to shake down.

"You are putting me in a bad place," I shouted. My voice trembled.

The conversation could only go so far. My roommate was at work. He refused to engage in my upset. He told me we would talk about this once he returned home for the night. To which I responded, "You are darn right we are going to talk about it."

The fire pulsing through my body pushed me deeper. I lost my head and began running through the house, screaming, plotting how the next few days would go. It would be on my terms, and those terms were not negotiable. My emotions hit an all-time high, and as my feet hit the basement floor, I heard the words, "Stop! Brandon stop!"

My knees quickly hit the floor. God was speaking to me. It was my job to be still and listen. If anything wasn't negotiable, it was this.

"What are you doing?" the voice said. "How do you think this is right?"

My answer was, "It's not."

"You have asked him to go to church, right?"

I had. He declined.

"What kind of man, what kind of Christian behaves in this way? How will it look if you treat him in this manner? If you treat him with disrespect and call him names in anger then you are no better. You are a hypocrite in his eyes."

One of those massive defining moments that smack you dead in the face and make you pay attention had arrived on my doorstep. With a heaving chest, I continued to listen.

God asked, "Why are you so upset? What is it that you are so worried about?"

Deep down I knew what was troubling me. I didn't want to admit it, fooling myself into believing I could hide my thoughts from God. The words turned over in my head.

Money—I was worried about money.

His rent money, five hundred dollars, was already included in my budget, and now it wasn't going to be coming my way at all. The reality was God knew I didn't truly need the money, but I had already spent it in my mind. I still believe I heard God laugh at how ridiculous it was that I was this upset.

He said, "Trust in me. I will provide. You do not need to worry. Have I not always provided more than you need? You always say you believe in me, that you will do anything and everything for me, but yet you worry. You doubt. You question. And, you carry this disbelief."

My hands were clenched so tight that my knuckles were turning white. My fingernails dug deep into my palms. My heart ached. I called out, lifting my hands towards heaven and I cried out, "I surrender it all to you. I trust you to provide. I believe in you. I know you will provide. I surrender it *all* to you."

My arms were extended, my fists full up and pointing at God. I believed. My arms moved back and forth from my chest to the heavens. I surrender. But I really hadn't.

My hands were balled into fists. I continued to squeeze so tightly my knuckles turned white again.

Then I heard God's voice again, this time, more clearly than ever before.

"You have done this so many times before, you truly deny me from within. You are just saying what you think I want to hear. It doesn't work this way. You cannot deceive me. I can see you all too clearly. You are not letting go and truly surrendering."

My hands shot back towards the heavens and said, "Look, I give it all to you."

With a sternness that caught my attention, I heard, "Look at your hands. When you are lifting them to profess you are letting go and surrendering, your hands are clenched. To give, you must open your hands and release. For so many years, I have watched as you proclaim you are living for me and yet every time your hands are lifted to the sky your hands are clenched. You are not letting go. You are holding on. I'm trying to accept your surrender, but you are pulling it all back to yourself."

My heart raced inside my chest, wildly pounding so hard I could hear and feel it. God was right. I looked at my hands, actually pulling all my attention to them, and that is when I realized how tightly I was squeezing them together. Of course, God was right. I was not letting go. I was selfishly holding on to it all. With true conviction, I realized I had been wrong all this time. My heart, along with my hands, opened up as I boldly confessed my sins. With every ounce of my soul, I surrendered.

Blood surged through my veins, bringing back the feeling to my lifeless fingertips that had been clenched so tight that they were starving for life inside them. As I reached up to go, this time with open palms, a tingling coursed to the ends of my fingertips and back through my body. I could feel the surrendering I had been lacking all this time.

I surrendered for the very first time in all of my twenty-nine years. At the time, I didn't know the first time wouldn't be the last. Until you've heard God speak, when things get so upside down that you hit your knees and begin to negotiate, you haven't even begun to scratch the surface of who you truly are. When you surrender, you are able to build yourself up all over again, this time with your feet planted solidly on the most important foundation. God knocks and makes you stronger than you've ever been before.

I realized then that while I had been following a faithful life, that I had welcomed God in, I had never fully surrendered to His will. I knew this was my truth based solely on how I felt in those moments. I had held control over everything, only fooling myself into believing I was living according to what God had set forth for me. I was wrong. I felt it in the release. My plans, my fears, my upset were all left on the floor next to my knees.

Then came a set of instructions. God said, "I want you to show me you believe and have surrendered by taking the very amount you are so upset over losing and placing it in the offering plate this Sunday."

179

After everything I just felt and experienced, I knew there was no negotiating with God. I would do as I was being called to do. Sunday couldn't come quick enough. But first, I had needed to clean up the mess I had created.

When my roommate arrived home later that evening, I was in the basement. He was darting upstairs; I'm sure trying his best to avoid me, and the confrontation I had promised would come. He had no idea what had transpired after our call ended. I called up to him. He told me he would be right back. Knowing he was avoiding the situation, I quickly shouted back "Hey, I just wanted to let you know that I cleared my schedule on the first so I can help you move. I figured with your dad's truck and mine, it won't take much time. You don't have much stuff."

He was shocked. The tension eased from his voice.

"You don't have to do that," he replied.

"I want to," I responded.

Sunday rolled around. I got up, dressed for church, and wrote out a check for five hundred dollars. I was asked to give one hundred percent of what I was fearful of losing. I did just that. When the collection plate was passed before me, I pulled the check from my wallet and dropped it in. I'll admit I've been guilty of digging through the larger bills I have on hand to find the singles and giving less than I should. Not this day; I believe I leaped at the offering plate. I couldn't wait to throw my check in. It felt amazing to surrender.

The following week I didn't think of those five hundred dollars I dropped into the collection plate until something that was too big to be a coincidence happened. I received a call from two different modeling agencies that confirmed a booking totaling the amount of fourteen thousand dollars. I thought to myself, "Wait, this can't be happening." The five hundred I was so worried about losing was now covered twenty-seven times over. The rent I was worried about losing was now covered for the next two years. God had truly blessed me.

As I was thanking God for this amazing blessing another one was about to be bestowed through prayer and conversation with Him.

"I'm ready to take these tools and skills I've learned in building and build a business to help others in their homes," I prayed.

The name of my business was delivered through this prayer. It would be called Homecierge, the concierge to homes, anything the home desires. I felt as though I was now being called to work with my hands and reach people where it would benefit them the most, in their homes. My father's tools became more than a means to repair a broken shower. They would be used to answer God's true calling for me. This new calling was placing me on the path that in the end would lead me directly to the place I was always destined to be.

Tools in the Toolbox
Tool #11: Surrendering
"We turn to God for help when our foundations are shaking, only to learn that it is God who is shaking them."
Charles C. West

Welcome to one of the biggest challenges we face in our daily lives whether we realize it or not. The idea and practice of surrendering is the one tool that will yield the greatest results. I mentioned that surrendering happens in many stages of life. For some, it happens in more than one area of life.

Think about the key element of surrendering for a moment. The action itself at face value seems simple. Surrendering is to give up control.

It sounds simple, but it's really huge, isn't it? You might be saying: you want me to surrender my biggest worries, the pieces of my life that keep me up at night and consume my waking thoughts, and just see what happens?

Yes, that is exactly what I'm saying.

Now, I will admit giving up control hasn't always been my strong suit, at least not until this experience happened in my life. Like you, the idea of giving something over, whether it be power or money, does have the ability to create a great deal of anxiety. It can even make your efforts in life feel fruitless when things are not within your comfort zone. Whatever the strain, when things feel out of control it becomes difficult to surrender to the idea that there is a greater and much bigger plan at work. But I promise you there always is.

There are two sides of surrendering. One is where it is best to let go, and the other is where we must push through and not surrender to the temptation that is so often thrown in our paths. Do you face encounters with temptation on a daily basis? Most of us do. It can be anything from greed, control issues, fear—the list goes on. Is it possible that those temptations are really God's way of calling you out and asking you to surrender to His will? If you think hard enough, you can see where you are asked to put this tool into practice every single day.

Let's address the first element—surrendering and letting go of the things that do not serve God and then you. When it comes to surrendering to that will, most are not as quick to raise the white flag of surrender as we would be to throw in the towel on something else. There is a reason for this, and it's called pride. As we discussed earlier, pride can be a very tough sin to overcome. No one is free of this sin. I know I'm not. Pride is often the number one reason why we do not relinquish control. In life, there is only one entity you should never try to outwit or overcome. Of course, I'm speaking of God. He knows if you are surrendering or not. No matter how you try to trick or fool yourself, you are unable to fool Him. Think about my hands. I said I was surrendering, but still I held myself back. Are there areas in your life that you say you are surrendering to a higher power, but your hands are still clenched?

Then comes the second element; I've spoken about this idea in nearly every chapter. God never wants you to surrender your morals or beliefs. I did not surrender when I was asked to do so in the modeling world. I did not surrender to my own desires when my father passed. I didn't surrender to the idea that I didn't have the knowledge to do something, like fix the broken shower. Instead, I learned, I grew, I expanded my horizons, and stood on solid ground. I stood in the place I knew I was honoring God. I surrendered to these notions because it is what we are asked to do when walking through this life faithfully. It's an action that must stay in the forefront of our minds and never allow the temptation of life to sneak in and steal our ability to surrender to the higher power.

This quote by Charles C. West says it all: "We turn to God for help when our foundations are shaking, only to learn that it is God who is shaking them."

When those big storms roll in, and everything starts shaking, don't question, "why me?" Say, "God, I hear you. I'm ready to listen." Ask where you need to be surrendering in your life. Let the ground rumble because you just never know what kind of blessing He has waiting for you on the other side of unclenched hands and an open heart. Have you surrendered today? Will you surrender tomorrow? What about the next day? It's amazing what life has to offer when you put this tool into action. If you are ready to make this commitment, Tool #11, Surrendering, is ready for you. Toss it in your toolbox and come along.

Chapter 13
A Role "Model"
"You must be the change you wish to see in the world."
Mahatma Gandhi

There is an often unspoken way to life, leaders versus followers. It's just the way things shake out. It seems those characteristics are breathed into you at birth. Sure, some of it can be developed, that is why we seek education after all, but true role models are simply born. We are all born. Therefore, we are all role models whether we choose to be or not. Others will look to you when you least expect it.

If you asked me to pinpoint the day I felt I first experienced stepping forward as a role model, I would have to rewind time thirty years. I would find myself in middle school. That is when I first joined the D.A.R.E. program. Their mission hasn't changed much since I was helping educate my peers on the dangers of drugs and alcohol. This role snowballed into a plethora of others, but there are a few moments where being a role model not only changed someone else's life, it changed mine too.

While I've already told you about some of my misdeeds during my college days, I did do a many things right too. I took on the hefty responsibility of being a role model as a big brother in my fraternity. This role is not only accountable for being a great example but also being present and helping the fraternity as a whole become better. It's also there to provide security to the little brother—that someone is always there to stand up for him, to guide him, and teach him how to be a great leader. Most take on one to two little brothers during their college years. I took on five. I say this not to boast; I say this because I understood the need to help encourage, inspire, and help nurture someone else as others had done for me.

Nothing could have prepared me for the importance of being the actual face of a role model. I was front and center of advertising as my modeling career began to soar. It's one thing to say you want to be a model. It's another to understand the ramifications behind your choices as a model. As the saying goes, "Sex, lies, and rock 'n' roll" sells. It always has and it always will—especially in today's day and age. When it came down to it, I knew I would only use my image to portray what I would proudly put in front of the world when I wasn't in a still frame.

This is the very reason I chose not to do alcohol or cigarette ads. My role as a model was in fact a role model. Everything I did was captured for the record, and I wasn't going to stand for something I couldn't proudly stand for.

After college, while I was back in Atlanta, I continued to build my modeling career and started making extra money training clients at the World Gym. Like any other gym, it's a revolving door, but every once in a while a particular person catches my eye. I happened to notice a young kid who started coming in on a regular basis. As a trainer, I had a habit of watching people workout, trying my best to offer assistance when needed. I introduced myself and learned his name was Yaacov. He was a high school freshman trying his best to be healthy and gain muscle mass.

Honestly, he was all over the place. He worked every muscle group randomly and had not been taught proper structure or discipline. I occasionally began showing him the proper form of certain lifts. That turned into me eventually training him and constructing a proper program.

As we began to train together, I had no idea what bonds were being created. Yaacov, Yaak for short, lost his older brother at a young age due to a sudden and tragic heart complication. Losing his mentor, his role model, his big brother at such a vulnerable age was extremely tough. Slowly, I began to fill that void of his brother's loss. It wasn't spoken about, it just sort of happened. I was just someone Yaak felt comfortable talking to. Our occasional talks turned into an amazing fellowship. Time went on. Yaak learned the ways and the art of body building. I learned I had played a role, one I welcomed, in someone's life when they needed it the most.

When I moved to Charlotte and settled into my home, I began attending a new church. Quickly impacted by the programs, I began working with a program called The Big Deal. The Big Deal was designed to reach the hearts of first through fifth graders. It was a huge undertaking, but one I'm still proud to have been involved with. We took over the gymnasium and turned it into the inner workings of a warehouse. I labored for hours faux painting plastic molded walls to look like a two-story brick facade. When I was finished it looked like real brick.

A fake water tower was erected in a corner. A massive movie screen hung on the back side of a massive window. It was created to look like the top of a warehouse. With a pulley system in place, the windows flipped, and it became the screen for viewing the lessons overhead. It turned into an amazing place for kids to come and worship.

To add an extra layer of excitement, I would hide high in the tower and put a grinder against the metal. The wild sparks drew the kids in. I loved how excited they would get each Sunday morning. There isn't anything better than a child coming to know and in return loving the Lord.

High school students volunteered to help run the video equipment in the back, and that's how I met a kid named Hudson. Hudson was a skateboarder—a cool kid, who had his head securely on his shoulders. He also just so happened to look up to me. I told him if he could gather a group of friends, I would lead a LifeGroup for them. He rallied the troops which included his bandmates.

Each week we would gather at my home and discuss life as a Christian. While the group was first set up to be a Bible study, we quickly began fulfilling our calling to be the church. As a core group of five, we served our community in a different capacity each month. I realized quickly I wanted this group to not only hear the word but see it in action. Within this example of Christ, they also learned respect for themselves.

As our bond grew, they began joining me in the gym. One, in particular, a guy by the name of Stevie, was very interested in improving his overall body image. He was a bit overweight and looked up to me because of my dedication to keeping myself healthy. I was happy to help him find a centered happiness as I had done with so many before him. From the minute our hands hit the weights, a spark was lit within Stevie. To this day, he finds merit in a healthy lifestyle and has chosen to make it his life work. He is currently studying nutrition at the University of Chapel Hill. He aspires to attend medical school and become a doctor.

While it may seem odd to some that being this type of role model would be so highly important to me, it goes back to respecting God's gift of life. Still to this day, Stevie claims that if it weren't for me taking him under my wing and helping him reach his fitness goals, he would not be in shape nor headed in the path he is currently on.

I quickly learned these same lessons I was imparting on the younger generation when I was their age. I realized I was blessed with a temple that God asked me to respect. I work out, cut out the majority of fried foods, gave up carbonated drinks, and used nutrition as a source to power myself forward instead of a way to break down my temple. We only have one life to live.

It doesn't make sense not to live in God's example.

When it came to the youth group, the gym wasn't enough, though. As I said, I wanted the five young leaders to understand how their light could make a difference outside of themselves too. At the beginning of the book, I explained that when people ask if I'm a Christian, I say,

"No, I'm the church." I began teaching my LifeGroup this message. It's easy to say I'm a Christian.

It's a very different calling to be the church. You are the church when you go out and satisfy needs in the community. The church was never just a structure during Jesus's day. He preached in the streets. He healed the wounded where they stood. He called them into the temple on Sunday. He took action. This is being the church. My LifeGroup understood, and we became models of and for Christ.

The group would call their friends. We would rally the troops and help local missions and charities. We were particularly fond of one local charity, and we helped organize Easter baskets for different age groups. We collected backpacks and stuffed them for kids who wouldn't have school supplies. Thanksgiving, Christmas, and Easter you would find us serving turkey, passing out meals, collecting toys, you name it; we were the church. We've made countless trips to help feed the homeless at our local food shelter. The seeds of serving the community grew in our group. By being a role model for Christ, I slowly began building future role models. It's something I treasure and find these days to be among some of my best life's work.

The greatest gift God blesses us with is our temple. It's with this body we are able to love, learn, flourish, give, and use our unique gifts and talents to lead and be in His image. I will say it again, "You must be the change you wish to see in the world." Gandhi's words have always resonated with me. It's funny how a few simple words can stick to your bones, sink in, and inspire you to be that change.

Tools in the Toolbox
Tool #12: The Temple

"Do you not know that your bodies are temples of the Holy Spirit, who is in you, whom you have received from God? You are not your own; you were bought at a price. Therefore, honor God with your bodies."
1 Corinthians 6:19-20

Our greatest gift is the body we are given. It is the temple of the Holy Spirit.

We are halfway through this journey of my life story and the tools we have collected thus far need somewhere to be stored when not in use. It's now time for me to explain the significance of a toolbox.

In its basic form, we all know a toolbox is where we place and organize our tools. It's the placeholder for our tools, so they are readily available when needed. It's an outer shell which protects the tools from the outside elements and keeps them locked away for safekeeping.

Your body, the temple, is your toolbox. Repeat this with me: My body is a temple, and it is my toolbox.

The reason I left this tool until now is because you needed a few foundation building tools to help you keep your toolbox organized first. Now that you have the tools to address and cultivate a solid foundation built in God's spirit of patience, acceptance, belief, and so forth, we must address how it all comes together. Besides, your hands are full of tools, and you need a place to keep them until another "job" comes up.

Caring for the temple is no different than caring for your actual toolbox. Think about yourself as a child. No matter how your life went, whether it was storybook or an uphill battle, it's likely you had someone to help guide your choices. You were given tools, shown how to use them or how not to use them, but were not always allowed to practice using the tools as you wished. As you grew older, you became more independent and began caring for yourself. Do you respect the tools you were given enough to care properly for the toolbox? Do you fall into traps that disrespect the temple God gave you?

Your body is the most amazing, complex organism in the world. I'm a firm believer in, if you look good on the outside, you feel good on the inside, and vice versa. I'm not saying everyone should look or be a model. That isn't what I'm saying at all. What I mean is, are you comfortable in your skin? Do you take care of yourself in all the ways God wants you to? Size and looks do not determine worth, but it's how you carry yourself that paints an image for the outside world.

With that said, we are a beauty-driven society. Our ideals of first impressions are tied to looks as much as they are tied to our words and actions. It's a sad state. Let's take this down to a more simple example. Imagine before you a set of three toolboxes. Any of the three could be yours free for the taking. One is brand new, shiny with five drawers, two large bays to lock items away, and a large top lid covering a storage area for the larger items. Next to this toolbox is a rusted, beat-up old toolbox that you're not even sure will open. Besides that, it is a wooden box that has no handle. You could throw your tools in if you needed too. Which one, based on first glance would you choose? Let's not try to fool ourselves—it would be the shiny new box that sparkles.

When you open that box you see a perfectly placed set of sockets, screwdrivers, measuring tape, a hammer, utility knife all placed in their separate compartments and aligned in order from smallest to largest. Each is shining, ready, and waiting to be put to use when needed. It's the perfect scenario, at least, that is what most people perceive, but it may not always be the truth. This is why you have to be careful about how you treat and use your tools as well so that they do not become damaged and rusted inside that perfectly shiny toolbox. The toolbox and tools must work together, because if both are not maintained properly the outer temple and the inner tools can be destructive to the other.

It's time we treat the temple equally both on the inside and out. If we are beat up on the inside, we show it on the outside. If we have God's shining light flowing through our soul, it radiates on our faces and out of every pore. Beauty does come from within. It may be an old saying, but how true those words are.

There is a physical level of caring for the temple as well. If you do not care for your temple, it breaks down. You must respect it, feed it nutrients, and care for your heart, lungs, organs, skin—any and all components of the temple. If we toss our tools into the box with little regard, we'll end up with dents and dings, some so deep they are not repairable. The same goes for our temples. We only get one body, one toolbox, one shot.

When we are being and acting as the church, people are seeking the toolbox they want to most identify with. We gravitate towards people we see as most like us, or towards those we most want to become. By neglecting our temple, both physically and emotionally, we are ignoring God's call to shine, to enlighten, and to bring people over to see what is in God's glory. We essentially push away our chance to be the church for someone else.

Take the extra time to organize your toolbox, lubricate the hinges, and oil the drawer slides, so the toolbox is always functioning. Keep your temple healthy through emotional wellness. Exercise, eat correctly, allow God's spirit to pour over you and oil your soul. If not, life gets rusty and disorganized.

You now have tool #12, the Temple, ready for the toolbox. Use it wisely and come along.

Chapter 14
Devil's in the Details
"Be willing to leave EVERYTHING behind in order to pursue God's plan for you."
Author unknown

Dreams are nothing more than unfulfilled desires. Those little pushes of purpose that come from within and above and create a stirring inside you that refuses to let go. That is until you take the steps to make those desires your reality. My reality was I had turned 31 and the massive drive to be on television wouldn't quiet down. In fact, it was downright relentless at times. I arrived at a fork in the road. Homecierge and modeling were both doing great, but deep down inside it wasn't enough. When dreams are destined to happen, they have a way of sorting themselves out eventually. That isn't to say hard work isn't involved because that is the furthest from the truth; it's just to say God has a way of being in the details.

I got a call from my agency in Atlanta. There was a highly successful landscaping and design show that was looking for a new host. This was the major leagues. The prominent network was looking to replace the current host, who was wonderful in his own right but his age wasn't connecting with the younger demographics they were trying to attract. They were looking for a younger, hip, knowledgeable host who could breathe new life into the show. My father's love for lawn care and his passion for maintaining it taught me more than enough to be the perfect fit for this new adventure before me. Add my ability to build a deck or a pergola and I leaped at the opportunity. The contract was close to being solidified.

At the time, I hadn't made a name for myself in the television circuit. There was a similar show already airing on a rival network. This show was hosted by a seasoned veteran in the horticulture world of landscaping and design. When the executives behind this new show heard the other was in its last season, and production was ending, the job was pulled out from under me and offered to him. Respectfully, this host had a following; I did not.

Suddenly, I was back to daydreaming about television. I went on casting calls, still hoping the perfect opportunity would present itself, but to be honest, the process was growing quite tiring. While the perception is that acting and modeling are nothing but playtime, it's hard work and a trying process at times.

Then came the move I had hoped for. Michael called; he was one of the talent scouts at my agency. He informed me that there was an enormous show about to come down the pipes.

They were looking for model-type carpenters and interior designers. I was both, but I knew my abilities and resume as a carpenter far outweighed the chance to be a designer.

The production was so big that casting was going to be held nationwide in six different states, and the name was being kept under wraps. This call felt different—larger, more national than anything I had been put up for before; I wanted in.

Upwards of one hundred thousand people would come to the table and make their bid for this show across those six states. Michael informed me I had been requested, and recommended I make the audition in Atlanta.

When I arrived, there were two thousand people at the call. I put my name down as the carpenter. If there is anything I've always known how to do it is to play to my audience. If the show wanted a model-like, hunky carpenter, then a southern hunky carpenter they would get. I arrived in a mechanic's shirt that I made sure was unbuttoned to show the top of my chest. The sleeves were torn off. I was in excellent shape at the time, and I wasn't afraid to use my physical attributes. If nothing else, it would be the way I could stand out from the next guy.

The casting went on for hours, but when it was my turn, I had something to prove—I belonged on T.V. When I walked in, I caught the eyes of a lady named Jennifer Sullivan. She introduced herself and explained the outline of what would be taped during the audition. It's generally the same: state your name, give your location and agency's name, and then you would be asked a preset number of questions to see how you responded on camera. At the end, Jennifer said, "That was great! I think you are everything they are looking for. Honestly, I can tell you know you're going to get it."

I smiled and kindly thanked her for her encouragement. Then said, "Thanks, but I've heard that before."

To which she said, "No, I'm serious. You have an amazing look. You're the all-American carpenter. I'm telling you; they are going to love you! You're going to get it."

I'll admit I ate up her words. It felt amazing to hear. I didn't want to get overly excited or confident in landing the role. Little did I know that Jennifer was not just another casting agent, she was the casting director charged with finding the next big star.

Jennifer said, "I have been doing this for a long time. This is what I do. When I say I know what they want and I know who I think is the best to do the job, I am rarely wrong."

My hopes were growing by the second. Still, I knew disappointment, and I was cautiously optimistic. I left the audition and immediately called Michael, my agent. Jennifer had already called. She meant what she said; I had a bona fide shot. Michael told me I was put on hold, to hang still, more information would come. And it did, in the way of Jennifer personally calling me.

"We have to go to another level. We still have other cities to go to, but Brandon, you are at the top of my list. I'll be in touch."

I couldn't believe my ears. This was bigger than anything else that had come my way, or at least, it felt that way. For three weeks, I waited. I waited for anything, a whisper or a shout to come to know what my next move would to be. The waiting was torture. Then word came from Michael.

"You have a callback. Answer your phone when it rings. Jennifer is going to call you personally."

With trembling hands, I did answer that call.

"I told you; I told you," Jennifer gushed excitedly.

The next round of auditions was to take place in New York. This was different. I wouldn't arrive to another crowd of two thousand, this was intimate. The playing field had been narrowed significantly.

Jennifer explained the audition process. I would go on camera opposite an actor playing a would-be homeowner. I was to come prepared to interact with and teach a D-I-Y home project of my choice to the homeowner.

"We won't have tools," Jennifer informed me, "So bring what you will need."

This was post 9-11—it wasn't exactly like I could carry a saw on a commercial flight. I had to come up with a fail-proof plan. After a bit of strategic planning, I knew what I needed to do to land this role.

I would take an old frame, something with character and detail, and teach the homeowner how to repurpose it into a mirror for their home. The project was simple enough I could explain it quickly and yet unique enough that the lesson would be heard and remembered. I would have three options for the homeowner to select from. The only problem was I couldn't pack a mirror in my suitcase without the risk of it ending up in a thousand little shards. It didn't seem wise to try to carry it on, so the only option I had was to buy a mirror once I arrived in New York. My plans were coming together.

Touching down, I knew what I had to do, find a mirror. I went to a large home improvement chain. After searching feverishly I realized they not only didn't have a mirror that would work, they didn't even have the ability to cut glass in the store. Things weren't panning out. The next logical choice would be Plexiglass, but even that fell through. I couldn't believe that the one time I needed a simple mirror I couldn't find one in the city that is known for having it all. Time was running out; I would have to go to the audition without the mirror. I began to recalculate my plan in my head. By the time I made it to the two-story walk up, I had regained my confidence.

The audition was upstairs in unit 220 if my memory serves me correctly, but lo and behold, downstairs in 128, you'll never believe what occupied the space—written in large bold letters the sign read King David Gallery, Custom Mirrors. I looked at my watch. I had just enough time to see if I could get a mirror cut and make it upstairs to the audition.

I rushed in and asked the man behind the counter, who also just so happened to be the owner, if he could give me a price on a custom mirror cut. He asked what I was doing and I told him about the audition that I was about to have in the space right above his store. Furthermore, I said, "I'm going to change the world for the better. This is my chance."

I've already said I don't believe in coincidences. What are the odds that a custom mirror store would be located downstairs from the audition?

That little nudge inside to make my dreams come true had grown to a full-blown push. I felt my dreams turning into the reality I so desperately wanted.

I told the owner I didn't need anything big, just an 11x17 cut would work, but I needed to know the cost. All he had in stock were huge pieces of continuous mirror. I knew the cost would be higher if he had to cut a small section and potentially lose the ability to sell the entire piece. Without relaying the cost, he popped the mirror with his knee and made the cut. I immediately said, "Wait! I asked for a price first; I don't know what you're going to charge."

The store had a great old vintage cash register with big round buttons. The kind that is more to store the money than keep track of sales. The owner kept pushing buttons. Inside, I grew nervous. With so many numbers being calculated I was worried I had just bought a mirror in the amount of my monthly mortgage. Finally, the keys became quiet. I looked at the aged glass at the top of the register where the price was displayed. On black-carded backdrops, white numerals read $0.00.

"I'm confused," I said quickly, "It says zero."

"What, is that not fair?" he questioned.

"Well, I mean, I want to pay for it," I replied.

With a smile and a blessing, the owner said, "How do you put a price on something, on somebody that will change the world?"

I was overtaken by emotion. He had just damaged an entire mirror for an 11x17 square. An 11x17 square that really did have the potential to change not only my world, but others'. Gratefulness and disbelief turned to fierce confidence. I watched the owner finish the mirror, sanding the sharp edges with wet sandpaper. I knew I would add this to my routine once I made my way upstairs. I wished he knew what an impact he made on me that day, and perhaps he did.

With the priceless mirror in hand, I was ready.

At the top of the stairs, a clearly nervous girl was waiting.

"Are you the only one here?" I questioned.

"There is someone inside," she replied.

We made small talk. She was there to audition as a designer.

The door opened and out stepped Jennifer Sullivan. She was escorting the last carpenter out of the door. She saw me, smiled and said, "Brandon! Wait right here."

She closed the would-be designer and I back in the hallway. I asked the designer if she knew what the show actually was, as it was still a tight-lipped secret. She didn't have a clue either. When the door opened, Jennifer beckoned me inside.

From the moment I began, everything felt right. The man who played the homeowner was a natural jokester. He

purposely tried to derail my focus, but it was razor sharp.
He joked, and I played back. My accent is thick. It became
his next target, mocking my words and my southern drawl.
The banter was amazing, and the executives sitting in the
room were laughing and eating up the charisma pulsing
through the room.

Jennifer had scheduled me last. I had no idea how
many had stood in that same spot or how long they were
allowed to speak. I was in the room for nearly thirty
minutes. When my time ended, I knew I had given it my
all. Jennifer walked me out.

"There are no guarantees, but Brandon, don't leave."

The same pretty designer that was waiting when I
arrived was still sitting on the bench.

"No one has been in that room longer than three
minutes," she smiled. "Nor did she say goodbye to anyone
else."

The "she" she meant was Jennifer. After returning to
the hallway, Jennifer pulled me into another room and
closed the door. You killed it!" she said, "They love you!"

No decisions were made that day. I would leave New
York not knowing whether I would be the future southern
carpenter on a national show or if I would be a southern
carpenter in my hometown. When you are waiting to hear
about something you want so bad you can taste it, time
moves incredibly slow. Weeks turned to a month, and no
one had heard a word. My agent didn't know anything.
Since I had built a rapport with Jennifer, I called her to see
if she had heard any news or had any updates. She hadn't

heard of any decisions yet either. She didn't actually work for the network. She had been hired to place the talent for that particular show, nothing more.

I turned to a conversation with God. It was me who did all the talking this time. I told him that if I am to be on a show, I knew it was to be this one. They loved me. This was it. But, if the call doesn't come I would continue to grow my business and know that this isn't what you want for me. For me, it was settled. The boundaries were set and I thought I knew how God wanted me to move forward.

A month slipped into two, and then three, then four. By then, I decided I would give up on hearing the news I thought should have already been delivered. Still, like surrendering, I said I was giving up, but internally I prayed. I talked about it. I wanted to be on this show, whatever it was. I had a good feeling about it. This *was* my chance to change the world!

For eight months, I built up Homecierge by truly doing anything and everything inside homes. I expanded my knowledge and skills in all areas. All the while I had been letting the devil slip into the details of my world. I had to admit to myself that this was all I had ever wanted. I began to question why the offer hadn't come. This was my chance, my shot to use this stage to show people what a Christian soldier really looked like. That role model God had set me up to be, I would be able to reach people in a way I hadn't ever been able to do before.

My business was doing well, taking off in new directions every day. I allowed the doubt growing inside me to talk to my heart. I convinced myself that this was all there was for me. I didn't get the show because that wasn't what I was supposed to do. God told me so. I had this opportunity before, and it never fully worked out. This wasn't in my cards.

When my hope was lost, I began to bargain. I took on a new client. They needed help with their master bathroom remodel. By now, I was a pro at these sorts of things. The job was simple—redo the tile and the shower. It was a bit of déjà vu. Things weren't lining up and going the way I expected with the remodel. I was growing more frustrated by the minute and then my phone rang.

Joy, another talent scout within my agency, was on the line. A request came for me to attend an audition the next day.

I scoffed at the idea. Between the aggravation of the bathroom tile and the thought that God had already told me to stop chasing this same line of pavement that was leading absolutely nowhere I lost my cool.

"Let me ask you something," I bitterly said, "Do they want a male or female?"

"I don't know," Joy replied. "They don't know yet."

"I'm not interested. You call me when they want a six-foot-two man with an olive complexion, dark hair, an athletic build, and until then, I'm not wasting my time chasing these auditions. I don't want to be a part of the cattle call. I'm done. I need to focus on my business."

Joy was taken aback. She didn't know what to say. She offered to take me off the rotation and to stop sending me out for jobs. In a moment of irritation, I said, "You just do that," and I ended the phone call. I went back to work and guilt set in. I had no business speaking to Joy the way I did. It wasn't her fault things weren't working out with the one thing I wanted more than anything. It wasn't her fault the tile wasn't lining up the way it should. I tilted my head up, raised my left eyebrow as to ponder at God and I said, "I'm right, right? You said if I didn't get this show, if it didn't work out, then this wasn't my purpose and my calling. I'm not going to go crazy chasing this dream. Right?"

I continued to speak, when I heard, "But. I. I can't get a word in edgewise."

I stopped. As I had heard many times before, God was answering my question.

"I never said that. You told me that was the plan. I never told you this isn't what you are supposed to do. You are putting your words in my mouth."

I quickly interjected.

"God bless me with this show, and I will bless you tenfold in return."

God sternly replied, "Therein lies your problem. You continue to try to negotiate with a non-negotiable item. It doesn't work that way. It is you that is to bless me and in return blessings may be bestowed. I never said discontinue the climb toward your dreams and desires. You must never underestimate the power of Satan. He takes great pride in preying upon your greatest insecurities. He removes hope and destroys dreams. He is using this to fool you in my name. You had a conversation with a self-righteous faith and I wasn't in that conversation. You are forgetting that I'm the one who is in control. You are not in control, but I am. You need to let go of your insecurity over your image, your pride, and conceit and using your looks to your advantage. You have to surrender the way you idolize yourself and your self-image. You and I are not equal nor are you better than me."

Immediately, I felt the conviction of the truth he was speaking to me, and I broke down.

"You are absolutely right," I said.

I was scared. This was truly the one thing I have always wanted. That mustard seed that had been planted so many years before by Professor Pilkington had been growing inside me out of control. I wanted to taste the fruit of that seed more now than ever. It's all I wanted. The devil knew it.

I heard, "You must surrender your whole heart to me."

My hands were not clenched this time. This time, it was my heart. I could feel every beat profoundly in my chest. My heart felt restricted like it was being strangled from beating again. I realized at that moment what my heart truly desired was where my greatest struggle to surrender was, hidden deep within my heart. It was then I surrendered my heart fully to God and proclaimed my faith in his image. It would no longer be placed within my self-image, but his.

"I really do trust you. I promise never to give up on this pursuit. I trust you. I promise I will never quit.

Whatever you give me, I will bless you. I will be your light. I will be your church."

Knelt down in someone else's master bedroom, I realized when I surrendered the first time I surrendered my insecurities over financial matters. What I didn't do was surrender my insecurity in my personal conceit. I had continued to put myself above everything and everyone, including God. I would be the church he called me over and over again to be. That would be the blessing he asked me to be.

I picked up the phone and called Joy back. This was a Monday. I told Joy I couldn't come to Atlanta now, but I would be there on Wednesday at four p.m. I apologized for my words. She was more gracious than I deserved. Before I hung up, I said, "I'm going to get this one this time." I had a newfound freedom and peace. I relished in it.

I spoke with the homeowners, shared my opportunity with them, and they told me to go. I promised to complete their remodel by Friday of that week. If I were going to make a place for myself in this world, I would have to go through the entire process. The next day my phone rang again. This time, it was Michael, my agent. I figured he was calling to talk to me about my conversation with Joy and tell me more about my call the next day.

I started the conversation with, "I'm going to be there. I'm coming down tomorrow."

Michael said, "You can't. You don't need to come tomorrow."

Sadness found me. I missed the casting call. They had already settled on what they were looking for. I had missed my chance.

"They didn't even let me try," I said.

Michael laughed, "No, that isn't it at all. They are still having auditions. I said you were not available."

"What do you mean?" I questioned. "Why not?"

"Because," he paused, "You are the new carpenter on *Trading Spaces*."

Numbness hit. "Like TLC, Trading Spaces?"

"Yes," Michael said.

"That's the biggest home improvement show in the world!" I said.

"Yes, now, I want you just to enjoy it. I'll be in contact."

I was overwhelmed with emotion. It was the very first time I understood what tears of joy really meant. What they truly felt like. They are soulful and deep. They come from a place that's beyond you. My heart was open and filled with God's presence. I had been so constricted for years and here was my moment.

Looking up to God, I swear I heard him laugh. Here was the definition of tenfold blessings. This wasn't just any show, this was a wildly successful platform to build the foundation of my calling upon. It was Godly faith that I had achieved in those moments with God. I had achieved the truest and most solid foundation. I knew it could never crack because I had surrendered my heart.

Tools in the Toolbox
Tool #13: The Art of Blessing
"With pride, there are many curses. With humility, there comes many blessings."
Ezra Taft Benson

Have you ever been blessed? It's a broad question. A blessing doesn't have to come in a grand fashion, it can be as simple as the car in front of you paid for your morning coffee before you made it to the window. It's a welcomed and unexpected blessing. Another small but meaningful blessing could be that the person at the grocery store check-out notices you have only one item while their cart is overflowing and tells you to go before them. These types of blessings, while small, are just as important as the momentous blessings that we experience and hold dear.

In their most basic forms, blessings are selfless acts intended solely for the betterment of the person the blessing is intended for. It's important to note, a blessing is never a true blessing if it is done to benefit yourself. Think about the differences between a blessing and a favor. A blessing is selfless. A favor is often done with an expected return.

Getting this basic fact wrong could cause undue stress or even put your life in a holding pattern until you realize that you must bless in order to be blessed. There is an art to this tool, after all. My idea of what a blessing was and how it should have come to be was all wrong when I asked God to bless me. I wanted something in return for giving something to Him. As I was told, "it doesn't work that

211

way." The reason I said I felt God laugh was because there I was again trying to negotiate with a non-negotiable item. Our blessings from God come just as our earthly blessings do. It's a circle. You bless Him in his glory then He will bless you in return.

God promises that if we concentrate on blessing Him and others, he will always take care of our needs. Think about this as well: you cannot out-bless God. The more you bless others in His name, the more blessings He pours onto you.

Learning the true meaning of a blessing is more rewarding than any blessing you will ever have a chance to receive. It's an immediate feeling that brings warmth and comfort into your heart.

Also know, as I have explained, that if you choose to do the right thing and stay strong to your morals that is a form of blessing others. The people in your life are witness to a daily blessing through your example. Understand not all blessings come from specific acts; sometimes you bestow a blessing onto someone with the simple gift of love, respect, friendship, or even a hello, when they need a smiling face.

The number one rule and key to being a blessing is never expect anything in return. I cannot say this enough because so often we blur the line between wanting something and being a blessing. My mother never wanted anything in return for helping the hospice care facility with their silent auction, but she was blessed years later with a comfortable place for my father to pass. The blessing our family received was tenfold what my mother did. Bless and then be blessed.

Think of all the ways, big and small, that you can be a blessing to those who are in or impact your life. Approach the blessing selflessly. Do not consider any deed too small. If you feel drawn to do a good deed, do it without hesitation. Look to God for answers. Ask Him what blessings He would like you to bestow upon Him. Each day think to yourself, *have I been a blessing*? Practice this art, this tool, to make the world we live in a much better place.

If you are ready to be a blessing, you now have tool #13, the Art of Blessing, ready to use.

Toss it in your toolbox and come along.

Chapter 15
Are You a Believer in Unlikely Spaces?
**"When His truth is at the core of your existences—
strength flows into every other area of your life."
Ephesians 6:10 - 18**

With my dreams coming true, I had a profound desire to share the news with the man who first planted the seed, Professor Pilkington. If anyone would be excited and proud of me, it would be this man.

When Professor Pilkington returned my call, my first attempt landed dead-smack in the middle of Sunday lunch; I told him how he planted the seed all those years before, and I wanted to thank him sincerely. He was kind, as he always has been, and said, "I appreciate your call, but this has always been your destiny. I'm glad you finally found your stage."

And what a stage it was. In case you weren't one of the millions who tuned into *Trading Spaces* every week, the show's concept was an intriguing one. In each episode, two neighbors would, well, trade spaces. Each episode was made up of a two-person team who had two days to remodel a room on a strict budget of a thousand dollars. They were not on their own, however. With a designer as their guide and a carpenter, like yours truly, the team essentially flipped a room in their neighbor's house. The catch was the homeowner had absolutely no say in what happened in their home. Teams were forced to stay away from their spaces and were only shown their new digs during the big reveal at the end of the final day.

The show ran for eight seasons, from 2000 to 2008. My first day was in 2007. During my first episode on the iconic show, I was paired with designer Frank Bielec during a sweltering summer week in San Francisco. Frank is as kind and sincere in person as he appears on television. He instantly put me at ease, and we got to work. Soon *Trading Spaces* was my home away from home.

At one point during my time on the show I was asked, "So, are you just a pretty boy or can you build stuff too?" It was a harmless jab, one I'm certain the person was asked to say, but I wanted to be taken seriously. I was there to build, to be a carpenter, to be an artist, and to be more than a pretty face and the nickname that would come with my days on the show.

Behind the scenes was a flurry of activity. While you may have only seen a host, two designers, a couple of homeowners and me, like all home improvement shows there was an entire crew behind the scenes working to create television magic in two to three days. There was no way any of us could have done the job we did without the support staff.

Like I said, my first episode took place in an all-out heat wave in San Francisco. The heat was making it impossible to work. The background carpenters, knowing they would not be on television, took their shirts off to catch even an ounce of relief. That became an expectation for me too. They were able to hide in the background, but I wouldn't be afforded that same kindness.

The producer came to me and said, "You need to take off your shirt."

I refused, politely. The rumor mill had already circulated and buzzed in my ear. A previous designer had pulled the same antics, and he was never in another episode. I'm not positive that was the reason he lost his job, but I wasn't going to risk it.

The producer pushed, feeding me the line of what to say, "It's hot out here. I have to take my shirt off."

When I refused again, he sighed, irritated I wasn't following orders, and said, "Oh, please, what do you think you were hired for?"

"Because I'm a good carpenter," I snapped back.

God and I had an agreement, a sound deal; I would not idolize myself, nor would I fall back into conceit. Those details where the devil laid were coming back to ask me where I stood. I knew I would have to play the role I was hired for, and keep my head on my shoulders while doing it.

Of course, as a model, I wouldn't be allowed to take off my shirt as any normal guy would by pulling it over my head from the neck. Instead, I had to start from the bottom and slowly pull it over with my arms up as to not hide my body. I hated every single second of that moment. It made me uncomfortable. I wanted to do my job without the distraction of a few muscles. Being new, I didn't want to buck the system. It wasn't like anyone hadn't seen me without my shirt on before. All a homeowner had to do was head to the computer, and any number of my modeling photos would be on display. I did as asked. Still, it was embarrassing. Every single scene had to be shot with my shirt on and my shirt off. While the camera drew in and essentially set me up for the viewers to follow me with or without my shirt on, it still felt wrong. After the second episode and seeing the editing that was slowed down and the most inappropriate music added into the scene, I respectfully said no. Building God's audience and a bookcase could just as easily be done with my favorite t-shirt on. Two episodes in and I already had a nickname— "the shirtless carpenter." Trust me, it's still a name that follows me, and now one I find to be quite humorous.

The show begged viewers to expect the unexpected at every turn. Whether it was sand on the floor of a basement or hay glued to the wall, it drew people in. But so often the unexpected happened behind the scenes too.

A year or so before I landed this role, I had purchased a worship ring. A man I greatly respected wore one and I felt like it was the greatest way to symbolize not only my love for the Lord but also to remember to keep him in everything my hands touched. Despite my hands becoming rough and beat up, that silver ring never left my left hand. This included when I was on *Trading Spaces*.

The word worship would catch people's eye. It would beg them to ask the next logical question: Are you a Christian? That simple question opened the door to the stage God was building for me to glorify him. I cannot recall how many times that question came, but it was often. I was able to express freely my love through my carpenter's hands.

There is a fine line when it comes to business and glory. I knew my place and knew what was and was not proper to say on the set. Again, not pushing my faith unless asked. I knew my worship ring was reaching people, so too were my actions. Both were simple things, but it's the little things and actions that often open the biggest doors. I made a promise to glorify him in everything I do in that master bathroom covered in unfinished tile.

The clearest moment of this glorification came in the most unlikely way and space in Colorado. It was also the justification that I knew God had placed me where he wanted and needed me to be.

Trading Spaces was never scripted per se; we were given points called a beat sheet to keep the show moving and on track. This particular episode pitted a boss against his assistant. The two were best friends. They had been working at the same business for a very long time. As promotions took place, one of the men surpassed the other and that changed the balance of the relationship. The couples got along well, both inside and outside of the office, but in the months leading up to the show things changed. No one could quite put their finger on the tension, but still there was a massive elephant in the room. Everyone could feel it, but we placed our assumption on the problem in the wrong place.

I was working with the boss's family. The boss wanted to make sure his assistant knew how much he appreciated him and that they were friends first and foremost. Designing a new space for him and his family didn't seem like enough. He wanted to show his appreciation with a cake. Knowing what a huge Denver Bronco fan his buddy was, we set off to build a cake stand shaped in the form of a football and the number one. He wanted to show him while he was honoring his love for his buddy's favorite team; he was really telling him he was number one to him.

While I was downstairs in their basement working on other projects, the wife came down to assist me. We began chatting, and the conversation began to flow easier than anyone expected. It had already been said that the two couples hadn't been around each other as much as they had been in previous years. We all assumed that it was because the assistant was now uneasy that his best friend was also now his boss. It seemed logical and well within our human emotions to have a bit of jealousy or even resentment for the shift of events. The beat sheet prompted me to ask a question that would change the entire realm of the show.

"So, do you miss the time when you hung out all the time," I asked.

The wife nodded. She did miss their time together, but she said, "It has to do with their children." Then she became upset. "She is really busy with her children. It's their world. We understand."

I was confused. The tears were beginning to flow down her face. Her emotions were raw and the cameras were rolling.

"What's wrong," I asked, trying to console her.

The conversation went on. By now, her tears were rolling, and she let us all in on a secret that not only was devastating to her and her husband, but everyone present felt their hearts break for them.

"We haven't been able to have children," she uttered.

That was the so-called problem between the boss and his assistant. It wasn't their work relationship; the heart of the matter was the boss wanted the life his assistant was building. The entire show changed at that moment.

"There is a plan," I said. "There is always a plan, trust me."

I found myself standing on my faith, that rock-solid foundation, to get us all through the next moments.

"Is that why you are not around them as much?" I asked.

"Yes," she nodded, "It's hard for us to see how happy they are. It's hard. It hurts."

While I couldn't be certain, something told me that at some point they would have the child they so desperately longed for. We wrapped our arms around each other, and I let her cry. Sure, it was a television show, but in those moments, we were changing the definition of someone's life. We were placed in our positions to lead and care for these people. I was the church. I didn't have to tell her I was a Christian. I didn't need to flash my worship ring. All

I had to do was show her and let her feel it. This was an extremely personal issue that most wouldn't want to share with the world while a camera rolled on their deepest desires, but she knew I was listening. These moments are what faith is all about.

This revelation was bigger than any revelation we had to offer. These couples were able to talk the matter through. It's funny what unsaid words do. One couple thought the problem was the relationship at work. One couple ached for their life. When everyone came to the table, a relationship had been given the tools and answers to be healed. You just never know when God will call you to serve. It's in these moments I am so thankful God placed me where he did. In the most unlikely space, a basement of someone's home, we were able to help another believer.

Tools in the Toolbox
Tool #14: Empathy

"The most beautiful people we have known are those who have known defeat, known suffering, know struggle, known loss, and have found their way out of the depths. These persons have an appreciation, a sensitivity, and an understanding of life that fills them with compassion, gentleness, and a deep loving concern. Beautiful people do not just happen."
Elisabeth Kübler-Ross

At some point or another, we all build walls and barriers around ourselves. While this act is often done subconsciously, they still exist. These walls are formed for so many reasons, whether it's from sadness, loss, tough storms, or even unfilled desires.

While these barriers are frequently tough to penetrate and even harder to knock down, there is one tool that does wonders when demoing the walls. That tool is empathy.

You know the old saying, "Put yourself in someone else's shoes"? This is the perfect example of how empathy works. The act of empathy helps us identify and understand what others are going through.

There is an important element of empathy that should not be misunderstood—empathy and sympathy are very different emotions and actions. While they are both feelings, sympathy asks you to feel for a certain person or situation. Sympathy is feeling sorry or having pity, but you do not have experience in relating to what the person is feeling; you have a degree of understanding of their plight. Empathy is best described as feeling with the person. Instead of feeling sorry, you can identify with the person's emotions, because you've experienced something similar. We all process our emotions in a different way therefore it's nearly impossible to be fully empathetic at every turn because each reaction, thought, and feeling is unique to the person.

When the homeowner spoke of her desires and inability to have a child at that point, I had empathy. I was able to break down her walls because of experiences that have touched those around me. I understood her emotions which allowed her walls to come crumbling down.

There are other ways to be empathetic and cultivate empathy in your life. Here you'll begin to see some of our tools overlap one another. Some tools are better when used along with their mates.

The first empathy-builder is to simply listen. You cannot be empathetic to someone if you don't take the time to listen and be present. This also takes active listening. That is listening without distraction or with placing our own feeling and interpretation on someone else's experience.

The next is to simply share. Empathy is a two-way street of opening up. Sharing your vulnerabilities, as I'm doing with you, creates an emotional connection.

Be willing to be active in a conversation without passing judgment. We share our situations and concerns with others because we are looking for understanding and respect. Passing judgment removes compassion and empathy.

Be courageous. In the same way we do not want to pass judgment, we also want to offer help when it is needed. It's okay to point out a wrongdoing in kindness if it will benefit the person and is done so objectively.

Give of yourself. Do this by taking an active interest in other people's lives. This breeds empathy.

Lastly, offer an ear, a kind word, and help when needed.

Ask yourself: do I have the ability to see the world the way someone else does? If so, you have the tool of empathy in your toolbox. If not, use the skills above to gain the tool of empathy. So many times empathy can help solve even the hardest of situations.

You now have tool #14, Empathy. Toss it in your toolbox and come along.

Chapter 16
Will You Answer When Called?

Ten years have passed since college ended. Ten years I had spent on the road modeling and spending days and nights with you in your homes via the television screen. Ten years since I had spent time at my most cherished stomping grounds, Appalachian State University.

A lot changes in ten years—a lot. My connection with my fraternity was still there. I received an invitation to attend that year's homecoming game, and I thought it would be an excellent opportunity to see how things had changed while I was away. Truthfully, I was anxious to see what had changed more, the University or me.

Homecoming was amazing under a brilliant sky. With the sun shining, it was the absolute perfect day for a game. It was amazing to plant my feet onto the ground of the one place that shaped me more than just about anything else. I had just wrapped *Trading Spaces* and episodes were still airing. While I was just a man returning to what was once my home, there was a buzz around me everywhere I went when on campus that day. I was no longer Brandon Russell, Delta Chi President; I was Brandon Russell television star. The stirring was a bit surreal. My success was their success, and I liked it that way.

I walked up to the fraternity tent at the tailgate party and was immediately greeted with a warm reception. With the music blaring, the smell of chicken and hamburgers circulating my head, the memories started coming back.

The new pledge class made their way to me and each introduced himself. They knew my name, and I wanted to know theirs. It was amazing to get to speak to them. I was home. I was in my element, and I came with a renewed perspective on the world. I wasn't the same Brandon the brothers before them knew. I had washed myself clean from my self-righteous nature. I felt different that day. In fact, I felt better than I had in a very long time—validation does that to a person.

Throughout the tailgate party, one pledge in particular named Parker Wade made it a point to connect with me. He wanted to know about my experience as a brother and what it was like back then. We talked for a bit, and I asked who his big brother was. He replied he hadn't received one yet. I told him I was certain an amazing big brother was in store for him, but I said, "Always remember, if you ever need anything, never hesitate to call me anytime."

Parker asked, "Do you really mean that?"

"Seriously, if you ever need anything I am always willing to listen and help if I can," I replied. I had no idea the gravity of my words.

I went back to the party, enjoyed a thrilling game, and the rest of the festivities. When it was over, I went home filled with another great experience.

A few days later I received a friend request from Parker on Facebook. Facebook was relatively new, and it most certainly wasn't a mainstay in my everyday life. I accepted the request and stayed in touch with him through occasional conversation. A few months into our online interaction, I noticed Parker was avoiding the subject of the fraternity. I picked up on it quickly and asked if he was planning on staying in the fraternity. There was a long pause and finally, he responded. The answer was no. He had depledged. Of course, I was curious why. I wasn't upset, but I wanted to know if something had happened I should have known about.

He was afraid to tell me, worried that I wouldn't speak to him anymore, but little did he know that is not within my nature. Quickly calming his fears, we began to talk about other topics in his life. At the end of our conversation, I once again made the offer I did the first day we met.

"My offer always stands. You can always call me if you ever need anything."

A year into our friendship, my phone chimed at 1:58 in the morning. I was awoken by the sound of the text coming through. The text was alarming. It read: I really need to talk to you badly, can you talk?"

Admittedly, in the back of my mind I thought, I hope he hasn't been drinking and that he really needed to talk. It was sleep talking because I immediately dialed his number. When he answered I knew something was desperately wrong.

His tone was silent and somber. It is one of those moments that stops you and creates a numbness that fills your entire body without permission.

"Parker?" I questioned, "What's wrong?"

Silence.

"Please, do not worry, tell me whatever it is," I urged.

While I listened, Parker opened a window to his world that I hadn't been able to see before. He was so upset, trying to speak but wasn't able to say a single word. It was more sounds than anything.

"Parker, take a deep breath," I insisted, "or I can't understand what you are saying."

He paused for a few minutes, breathing in and out to slowly regain his composure. When he finally was able to speak, words that instantly saddened me tumbled from his mouth, "I can't stand it here! No one likes me."

He was utterly miserable. He hated college life. He felt like a complete outcast and those feelings made it where he could no longer accept himself. For hours, we talked. We stayed up most of that night while he wept.

My heart ached and broke all at the same time. The emptiness, disconnection in life from himself and his peers, all the torture and misery his soul felt ate me up. My insides were screaming, why hadn't he called me before now? I told him to call anytime—to never hesitate—but he had. I would have helped him along the way, instead of here, at this place which seemed to be at the top of a massive mountain looking up while a storm rolled in. He was in danger of losing his footing. Regardless, what I felt didn't matter. I had answered the call and was there to listen.

I lent Parker what I thought he needed the most in those moments which was a listening ear. In the cloak of a darkened morning sky, Parker released all that he had been holding inside and set himself free of the massive burden he had to bear. It was then that I slowly started to sow the seeds of fellowship and confidence he needed to know he had within me.

Being a friend, a true friend, is more than just being there in the good times, it's about being there when they are at their absolute most vulnerable. I told him how important he was, no matter how he was feeling. I told him despite not feeling relevant in the world, there were people who thought otherwise, me included, but regardless there was only one that ultimately mattered.

I explained to him that he is perfect in God's eyes. That no matter what came God would never forsake him by thinking otherwise. As He does for everyone, He had created Parker in His perfect image. I told him he had so many years ahead of him to fulfill his purpose and the reasons why he was placed on this earth.

As Parker started to settle down, we moved into normal conversation. It's then he mentioned he felt it best to leave Appalachian State. It wasn't right for him. It would be better if he returned to South Carolina and looked into Clemson University. As anyone would, I reminded him that we cannot run from our problems. No matter what they have a way of finding and catching back up to us no matter our address. I asked for a favor. I wanted him to dig deep into what it was that truly bothered him and resolve the discomfort and hatred towards his own existence. We ended the call a short while later. The text that came at 1:58 a.m. ended with my heart hoping my words had made a difference.

Parker decided to transfer to Clemson and finish college in South Carolina. Our friendship grew each time we spoke. It seemed he was doing better, finding a passion and love for life that was so inordinately missing that night. He was involved with an on-campus ministry and fellowship events that built friendships that he was missing at Appalachian. During the summer of 2011, I mentioned in a phone call to Parker that I was going to be visiting some of my best friends in Debadu, South Carolina, near Myrtle Beach. Parker told me he was going to be close to there, working as a lifeguard for the summer. I told him I would try my best to come and say hello while I was in town. I wanted to see him and knew how well he was doing, but honestly, something else was telling me I needed to go.

I arrived in Debadu and had a couple of days of free time while my friends worked. I drove the short distance to visit Parker in person. We hung out at the beach while he watched over the safety of the vacationers. In between the blows of his whistle, we caught up on life. After dinner, we went and found our way to a thriving little hot spot with a cool vibe and great nightlife. We grabbed some ice cream and found a bench outside to lap up and savor the massive cones. Outside on that weathered wooden bench, we began to talk about his life, what he was doing, and how his plans were shaping up.

He was dating someone new. She lived down there too, but their schedules did not allow them a lot of time together. He was mainly going back to the guard house every night where he was faced with a keg full of beer and a hangover waiting in the morning. I wasn't judging him, but I did say perhaps that wasn't the best way to spend the entire summer.

That's when the part of the story that was left out so many nights before on the phone came rushing out. Parker wasn't including himself in the nightly drunk fest because he didn't want to get out of control. I questioned what he meant. There was clearly more to the story than he was at first letting on.

"What do you mean out of control? I asked.

To which he replied, "Well, you know after all that happened at Appalachian with the arrest and the nights I had blacked out."

I stopped him immediately.

"What are you talking about?" I asked. "You never told me anything about being arrested!"

"Are you sure? I am sure I did," He replied.

I knew he had never breathed a word of it to me. He went on to tell me why he had been arrested. In the end, it was due to drinking so excessively that he honestly did not know what he was doing most of the time. He was blacking out repeatedly.

"When you say blacked out," I said, "do you mean ten or fifteen times?"

Parker was quick to say, "Oh no."

I breathed a sigh of relief that my numbers were too high, but I was wrong.

He said, "It's probably been like ninety or more times, at least."

I could feel shock setting into my face. I am good at controlling my responses, but no one is that good. I was flabbergasted.

"Ninety or more times!" I replied. "Parker, that is terrible! You never told me this."

He was certain he had, but I knew in my heart this was all new. I asked more questions, dug deeper and he willingly answered.

"I am not a psychologist, but it doesn't take one to know you have a serious problem," I gulped. This was huge.

Parker knew he was an alcoholic. He knew he had to accept the truth without an ounce of denial to get better.

"I need help," he stammered.

Alcoholism ran in his family. His grandfather had the same issue. I explained it could be genetic and can skip a generation. Parker's eyes were filled with shame.

"You are right. I believe I'm suffering from it."

I immediately told him it was nothing to be ashamed of, but it was time to get help. I meant every word, every exchange we had as friends, I would help him in any way I could. As I did that night on the phone I told him God loved him so much, and this isn't what He wanted him doing in his life or to his life. This secret, this need, was destroying him from inside. We prayed on that bench while the world turned around us. We were the church right there in the breeze and cool evening atmosphere.

Parker has a huge heart for the Lord. I knew it was there the entire time; he just needed to believe in himself and erase the insecurities he carried inside. At that moment, I explained to him he was like a brother to me because we are in the same family as Christians.

"We are family, and I care deeply for you, like a brother. Again, know I will be there and help in any way," I said.

I could see the change in his eyes. I was fertilizing his heart with reassurance and the confidence he needed for everything to grow within him instead of around him. He made a commitment to himself at that moment that I was honored to share.

"Brandon, right now, from this day moving forward, I am never going to drink another drop of alcohol again."

I was happy to hear this proclamation. However I knew it wouldn't be that easy. He had to be realistic to reclaim control. If he was going to continue to live in a place that was readily offering alcohol at every turn, his recovery wouldn't be all that simple. He assured me, he was moving out.

The peace that came from Parker that evening was nothing short of miraculous, at best.

God entered his heart, blew the doors off the locks that concealed all the pain he had hidden away, and truly erased all the little desires and pulls to ever touch another glass of alcohol again.

His journey forward would be tough and long. The next couple of years were met with their share of struggles. There was anxiety with his new calling to pursue God in the highest form, but it was never eased with a drink. He disenrolled at Clemson and enrolled in a school for ministry. This is what he was being called to do. He wanted to lead the youth. His life was a living example of the word.

He was walking with happiness. He had surrendered his heart, but his direction and focus were still not clear and somewhat lost. Parker wavered back and forth and eventually left the ministry school. His parents grew tired of his continued change of mind. They were supporting him through his many career paths and school and still nothing was coming to a head. When he complained, they just didn't understand he was just unsure of what he wanted to do; I went against what he was hoping and I took his parents' side. I was supposed to be his confidant and his mentor, always on his side, but I needed him to know he had to stop running and figure out whatever was still grasping at his soul. God had dug in but so had something else.

"You need to face the truth. Find a path, pray for a plan," I urged.

When you are being called and used as God's vessel to help a life, you find something within yourself that you didn't even know was there. You, yourself, gain an overwhelming understanding that God is growing you and your path as much as you are helping someone grow theirs. When I speak with Parker, so often, it is a truly humbling and amazing feeling when I can hear the words leave my mouth but know they are not mine. They are God's, and He has used my body as His vessel to reach Parker when he needed God the most.

Six years into our journey as friends came the most humbling acknowledgment of God's work. It came via a post on Facebook in which my name was tagged. So often, I ignore those tags, but opening it up I couldn't believe the words before my eyes. Parker had laid his entire heart on the table for all the world to see.

The post read:

"I, too, had someone believe in me. As a freshman in college, I was searching for my place in this world. A man met me in the midst of my deepest depression. He reached out a hand in pure love. Patiently, he watched, in faith, as I walked further down the road of despair.

"Knowing that, one day, I would recognize his pure love for me. Love that is straight from the Father. Two years passed, and my situation was so gloomy that I couldn't see beyond my hurt and pain. On the verge of suicide, beating my Bible against my headboard and screaming at God, a voice came to me. The echo of words spoken two years prior by that same man. 'If you ever need anything, I'm here for you.' So I did something I had never done before. I took him up on the offer. It was late at night, and he answered the phone. All I could do was weep; two hours on the phone until I couldn't cry anymore. In my darkest hour, God showed me His love. Through a man who knew this love so well. Thank you, Brandon Russell, for believing in me. Six years now since the day you said those words. To all who've been impacted by what God has done in my life. Honor is due to the faithful servant who showed me who I am. Loved by the Father."

I may have spent those years fertilizing Parker's life, but in those moments, he returned the favor. I will continue to be the man who answers the call. I will be a faithful listening ear. I may have saved a life that night and in return his life and experiences have and will continue to save so many. When you are asked to answer the call, will you ignore it or will you answer?

Consider this; if you don't answer the call the person on the other end may not be alive to make that call again. It doesn't matter what time of day or night it is, answer the call. It just might be your calling.

Tools in the Toolbox
Tool #15: Listening

When I was a child, I remember being told, "God gave you two ears and one mouth for a reason. You should do twice as much listening as you do talking."

As an adult, I cannot think of a truer statement. This is a tool you can never use too much.

This tool is a gift not only to yourself, but it's one you can give to someone else. If we do not listen how will we know someone else's needs?

When a baby cries, you know it is because there is a need that needs to be met. The same goes with people. When someone speaks, they are doing so with the idea that they are communicating their needs, ideas, hopes, and desires. There are times too that we speak to release a burden and find comfort in knowing someone else shares in our concern. As was the case with Parker the night he called. I had to listen to him to know what he needed in those desperate moments.

There is another valuable lesson as Christians I want to express in regards to listening.

That pertains to listening when in prayer. I have mentioned several times throughout this journey of the times I have spoken to God. When I've relayed these stories to others I often am asked if I speak directly to God. I always respond, "All day, all the time." I have conversations with Him daily.

There is a difference between prayer and a conversation. So often when people pray all they do is talk. They relay their desires and wants but never take the time to listen to hear what God has to say in return. A conversation is not a conversation if only one person is speaking.

Open your ears. I'm proud to say I speak with God in all that I do. I don't only speak to Him in times of stress or turmoil; it's an open line of conversation all day, every day. Many only pray when things are hard and upside down. I challenge you to have an open conversation with God many times a day. You never know what is waiting for you if your ears are not open.

Ask questions with the intention of listening for a response.

Take time with others. Listen feverishly in good and bad times. Not every life-changing communication comes when life is hard. People know when you are listening. So does God. Are you a good listener? Are you a great listener? Or are you just a good speaker? I dare you to create a balance.

If you are ready for open communication, you now have tool #15, Listening, ready to be used fully. Toss it in your toolbox and come along.

Chapter 17
Who Are You When No One Is Looking: Fix It Forward
"Give, and it will be given to you. Good measure, pressed down, shaken together, running over, will be put into your lap. For with the measure you use it will be measured back to you."
Luke 6:38

My first season of *Trading Spaces* wrapped. During the filming break, I returned to North Carolina and settled back at home. With the excitement of *Trading Spaces* and the skills I was able to share with homeowners across America, I felt compelled to take my skill set a step further. The promise I shared with the owner of the glass company in New York City before my audition for *Trading Spaces* still held true; I wanted to show my heartfelt gratitude and change the world. But that begged me to ask the question, "How?" That is when the concept for my charity Fix It Forward was born. With the business registered in 2008, I picked up my hammer and set off to help those in need.

Tapping into my childhood days of playing in the yard and knowing the names of all my neighbors, I quickly realized my national reach needed a hometown focus. Too many communities across the United States were and still are losing the center focus around how America was founded, on community. Besides economics, there is one main reason, at least in my mind, that this is happening. We have stopped coming to our front porches and have turned

into a back deck society. That is where the mission
statement for Fix It Forward came to be, "Resurrecting the
front porch community from the back deck society we have
become."

Simply put: neighbors do not associate like they used
to. Instead, we've fallen into the trend of building large,
private patios onto the back of our homes hidden away
behind a privacy fence and a jungle of trees to keep
everyone else out. Even arriving home for the night, we
pull into the garage, turn off the car, shut the door, and go
inside.

We have gone away from the days of welcoming our
new neighbors with a casserole, or helping with small
projects around the house. Somewhere between my
parents' generation and mine, we simply stopped asking
our neighbors' names. We've accepted a norm that allows
ourselves and everyone else to shut the world out. With that
comes the risk of shutting out the community. Granted, I do
understand that in many communities, fear of the unknown
beyond violence and social upset requires us to find
comfort within our four walls, but we are all missing out. I
am also aware that some neighborhoods possess some of
these old qualities, but on the whole that is slowly
diminishing. With the likes of social media and the lack or
need of upfront verbal face-to-face communication these
ideals are slipping further and further away.

If we do not stand on our front porches proudly, taking
a moment to enjoy the company of our fellow neighbors,
learn their hopes and dreams along with their concerns and

needs, we will never know about the people living right next door. Furthermore, how will we create a sense of community? This is my mission for Fix It Forward.

Fix it Forward establishes a grass roots movement. Our mission was founded to address one life-altering need per household. That need may seem minuscule to some but to others it is monumental. It could be that their kitchen needs to be updated due to run-down plumbing.

Perhaps they need a new sink and possibly a new refrigerator, or maybe it's that the bathroom is in absolute disarray, and it needs to be remodeled to simply function properly. Whatever the need, I, along with homeowners, complete the repairs so that if another issue arises, they now also have that valuable skill to help themselves or others in the future.

I mentioned a grass roots movement. Once the selected homeowner's project is complete, they are not asked to give anything towards the cost of materials or labor, but they are expected to Fix It Forward by choosing a neighbor on their street to receive the blessing of community help.

The idea and goal are to create a trend that keeps passing to the next neighbor until everyone in the community is served. As the neighbors of the community start to grow in number, the tasks start to shrink in time. With more hands on deck, the easier the fix, repair, or overall need becomes. This effort establishes a renewed sense of living while building community.

With education, God's will, and the ability to teach people how to create a solid foundation in life, I vowed, and still do, to resurrect the qualities in the front porch communities of yesterday.

While rebuilding a renewed sense of hope and community, the true fix comes from within.

Communities and individuals experience a transformation in their hearts.

As soon as the ball was rolling, I realized that not only was this an important community movement, this had legs to be a national movement too. Being the church, the hands, and feet of God, I wrote out the concept in hopes of taking this idea onto television too.

Let me stop there. My desire for taking this onto television was not to profit off the idea. I wanted to create a movement that took back our society and made people realize it wasn't my hands and feet at work, but God's.

Now, when Fix It Forward began, Ty Pennington had just landed and started filming *Extreme Home Makeover*. Being that the show was filming nearby a former producer from *Trading Spaces* that worked with both Ty and me called and set up a visit for me to introduce myself to Ty. I was thrilled. The red carpet was rolled out, and I was there to thank Ty for everything he had done to make *Trading Spaces* a success. We were both filming our own shows at the time, but I was in complete understanding that without the role Ty played on *Trading Spaces*, I would not have the comforts and success I was experiencing.

Once inside the VIP tent, a young lady recognized me. Her and her father came up to say hello. A friendly conversation was struck, and it led me to meeting his brother who was the home developer for that particular episode. We clicked.

I was asked the question I've been asked so many times, "Are you a believer?" I was honored he picked up on this fact, even though it wasn't something I had mentioned in the conversation. He went on to say, "I feel like there is something I'm supposed to talk to you about." I suppose you could say God was whispering in his ear. He invited me back to the set the next day to chat.

I gladly went. When I arrived at their trailer on set, I was met with six or seven people waiting. I didn't come with the intention to pitch Fix It Forward, but that is what happened. The developer was enthralled with the idea. He had personally helped raise funds for the house *Extreme Home Makeover* was constructing, and he knew we could take Fix It Forward's concept into the community. As he said, "I'm one hundred percent behind Fix It Forward, two hundred percent behind you." This type of support meant my small idea had the potential to be a mighty movement.

By the time we finished our meeting, the question was where do we start? The developer knew without a question of a doubt exactly where to begin, inside the house of Joy. Joy McGuire had been approached by *Extreme Home Makeover not* once but twice. Each time she missed out on getting the help she so desperately needed and deserved.

The minute I arrived on her property and came to know how Joy fixes it forward for her community, I rolled up my sleeves and wanted to help this woman and her family. Indulge me for a moment while I explain why.

Joy is truthfully an earthly angel. The woman has seen hard times. She is open with her words and the choices she has made in her life. Despite hard times and a desperate walk through darkness, she has committed her life to doing God's work. Standing on her porch, she founded her charity, With Love from Jesus Ministries-Charlotte.

Having empathy for the homeless, as she once was homeless herself, she has taken it upon herself to feed the poor not just during the holidays but every single day. Being the woman she is, she rolls out the red carpet, so to speak, during the holidays too. Without her, thousands of pounds of ham and turkey wouldn't help fill the stomachs of those needing help during Thanksgiving and Christmas. Her vision expands beyond that, however. Located behind her home and even in it, she has a makeshift grocery store and clothing area, where anyone in need can come, knock on the door, and gather the materials and nutrients they need to feed or clothe their families and themselves.

Everything Joy does is because of her love for her community and Christ. She also does this at the expense of her own well-being. Her living conditions are less than sub par. Not only is she an angel, but she is also a true soldier in God's army. Not many would be willing to put themselves in dire straits at the benefit of others. But that is who Joy is. Instead, she is a true steward of prayer and faith that God will always provide for her and others.

Unfortunately, Joy is often not left with enough to cover the expenses to maintain her home. And the home became broken. All of this while caring for a son with autism. Although she does it without a second thought, and in a way that somehow is seemingly effortless, I can't imagine the daily struggles that are placed on this splendid soul. I say this not to bring embarrassment, but to paint a complete picture of who this woman is. It is also to show that my movement could bless her the way she tirelessly blesses thousands of others.

I visited with Joy and asked her out of the many needs what was the one thing she wanted to be fixed inside her home. Truthfully, the house needs to be torn down. Our goal was to acquire the land next door and build a new home that would serve her and her family. While this was out of the scope of our normal concept, there was no one more deserving. In the meantime, we needed to do something to help with her current living situation.

I knew whatever she desired I would work to give her anything she asked for. Let's face the facts, anything she asked for had the potential to be life changing, but all she wanted was one simple wish. She wanted a comfortable and safe place she could relax. She needed and longed for a new bathtub. She told me, "I haven't taken a bubble bath in seventeen years. All I want to do is be able to draw a bubble bath and relax." Taking a warm bath is such a simple pleasure many take for granted, but that was all Joy McGuire needed.

With mold and broken fixtures, it would take a complete remodel of the bathroom in order to complete the project correctly. Armed with two thousand dollars, I set off to create the master bathroom of Joy's dreams. Still working on *Trading Spaces*, I knew I could make this project work on the budget I had. The space was tight, damaged, and uninhabitable, but a couple of weeks later, Joy had a working bathroom fit for an angel.

This project has been one of my most enjoyable ones. The fact that Fix It Forward could benefit someone so deserving is humbling. Joy was already fixing it forward within her community, but with the skills brought to her she had a new way to help.

The housing market was on the bubble when we started Joy's project. Prices across the nation had risen sharply. By the time we were finished, it had burst. The bottom fell out not only of the market but of my funding and partnership with the developers. They lost all they had—land, homes, developments—everything. It was a horrible loss for everyone. Fix It Forward was placed on hold and I returned to work on *Trading Spaces*.

This mission has and will always be my passion, and this is why. Not every home is in need of a million-dollar renovation. Not every thousand-square-foot home needs a ten-thousand-square-foot replacement. All the money being spent to add flash and glamor to a single home could be spread across an entire neighborhood and restore our hometowns. I'm not discrediting the charities, shows, or entities that make these types of dreams happen, what I'm saying is in the end what are we left with? One home, a few lives changed, when there is a community lying in wait for this same type of assistance. There is a grander scope here.

If we give and teach knowledge, we help others fix their needs. I also believe it is so important we do this on our own streets, here in America. We must start down the streets of Chicago, in the boarded-up windows of Detroit, the wards of Houston, my hometown of Charlotte, you get it, right here at home. As Americans, we tend to place ourselves on pedestals and act as these needs are invisible. We leave the work to charities and people like Joy McGuire. It's our job too.

I've been called to reach into our communities. To restart the grass roots our country was built on. Remember how our towns were created? We raised the local grocery, built the churches, paved the roads, and built houses around the community center. We greeted our neighbors. We knew their names.

I want to be clear that I believe in helping others when help is needed. I credit and commend all those who dedicate their time and do missionary and charity work overseas. It is greatly needed and must continue, I, however, feel I am personally called to focus Fix it Forward within American communities first.

Here is the perfect example of what I set out to create. If you have flown, you know that right before takeoff, the flight attendant instructs those in the cabin that in the case of an emergency the oxygen masks will drop. Once the masks fall, the first thing you are supposed to do is secure the mask to your own face first and then help your loved ones or neighbor next to you. If you run out of oxygen before you can help someone in need of assistance then you both suffer. We too often try to help their causes or countries while first neglecting ourselves. We are depriving ourselves and our communities that need us right here in America. This is my calling. This is why God placed this on my heart. One small seed can transform into a beautiful field. We have to harvest God's love back into our hometowns and on the broken streets. We have to fix it forward.

Tools in the Toolbox
Tool #16: Purpose and Calling

This tool, Purpose and Calling, isn't so much a tool as it is a basic understanding of the purpose for which we use our tools. We all have a purpose, a defined reason why God placed and keeps us on this earth. That's a beautiful thought, isn't it? You are here to fulfill a calling.

Joy's calling is to serve those who are unable to serve themselves. Your purpose may not be as defined as hers, at least not yet. I didn't understand part of my mission was to be a carpenter until my life was uprooted and my father passed away. Sometimes our calling doesn't shine like a giant beacon ahead. But I promise it's there.

If you are not living your best life, right this minute, then I know you are not truly fulfilling the purpose and calling God has created for you. The call waiting for you should create an inner feeling that gives you the extra skip in your step, makes your heart beat quicker, and makes you hold your head higher because you know you are fulfilling your life's work. Is that inner feeling there?

Have you heard the saying, "If you love what you do, you will never work a day in your life?" If you are living the calling God has set out for you then you understand this saying.

When you were younger, did you dream about a specific career or life that kept you moving forward and daydreaming? Are you doing it? If you dreamed of being a pilot who flies the transatlantic, why have you settled for something else? Where does your passion lie?

If you need a push in the right direction, there are ways to actively pursue your calling.

The first is the easiest: pray. Pray to understand your purpose and your calling. I bet you'll find the answer has been showing itself for quite some time.

Take notice of your dreams. Are you consistently dreaming of rushing into the Emergency Room and saving a person's life? Does that intrigue you? Instead of questioning the dream, question whether that is your purpose or not. God speaks to us in any way he can get our attention, that includes our dreams. If you have a hard time remembering your dreams, but you know you are missing something, keep a notepad and pen next to your bedside. You'll be amazed what comes during those sleeping hours.

Make a list. What do you enjoy? Would you rather spend all day baking instead of at a desk answering phone calls? Those urges and wishes are your purpose whispering in your ear.

Creativity requires time to be fostered; it is not always leisurely. Being creative could be your calling. I know it's mine, whether it's my passion for working on television or working in the community or someone's home, this is my calling.

What makes you curious? Have you heard about a field that captured your interest but you never took the time to explore it more? Is this one of those mustard seeds you should have been paying attention to?

Tap into your full potential. Without doing so, you'll never achieve a sense of peace because your mission is going unfulfilled.

Pay attention to what keeps coming back to you. Do you have a hobby or a habit that is your failsafe? Meaning, do you do something specific when you find yourself lost or stressed? Is that your true calling? Turn your hobby into your purpose.

Lastly, try to invoke that same tool that keeps finding its way into everything you do—patience. It took me thirty-one years to find what truly made me happy. Honestly, I would have come to know my purpose if I had allowed myself to be vulnerable and step outside of my comfort zone.

If you haven't found your true calling yet, don't lose faith. It's never too late to follow that inner call. Are you ready? Forget about what hardships could come your way. It's time to grow and live the life you were placed on this earth to share. Our talents are meant to benefit not only us but the world. Go ahead, tell me, how are you going to truly shine?

If you are ready to live a purpose-driven life, you are ready to use tool #16, Purpose and Calling, to its fullest. Toss it in your toolbox and come along.

Chapter 18
From Silver Tray to a Paper Towel: A Serving of Humility

Trading Spaces came to an end. It was an amazing run and even greater experience. My popularity on television had soared. During the height of those days, I found myself in Rockefeller Plaza appearing on the *Today* show. Other news stations were calling. This was a defining moment for me. *The Daily Show* with Jon Stewart had called. It was a big deal because it wasn't the norm to have a celebrity from my type of show on for an interview. The writer's strike killed the interview, but I can only assume he wanted me on to make fun of me for taking my shirt off in front of homeowners. I guess we'll truly never really know. It was still an honor to be asked. Everything I had asked for was raining down on me, and I wouldn't trade a single solitary second of it.

As filming wrapped with TLC, I patiently waited to be free of my contractual obligations.

Once my obligations were met, I was immediately picked up on another network. This time I was slated to be a host and a lead carpenter. This dream was happening not once, but twice.

The assets that *Trading Spaces* banked on, my looks, would finally not be the central theme of this new atmosphere. This show was more serious in a way. There wouldn't be a fun neighbor swap at the heart of each episode; instead we were tasked with rescuing homeowners from unfortunate situations. Whether it be a house almost finished being built that caught on fire, a bad contractor leaving behind a mess, a patio ready to collapse, or even lead poisoning from a painter who didn't protect the homeowner; whatever the catastrophe, we were there to right a terrible wrong on a nearly impossible deadline.

I was the first of the talent to be cast, then came the second carpenter, but when it came time to hire a designer for the show, things didn't pan out the way everyone was hoping. We shot a pilot with a designer hopeful. When the production company ran a test audience viewing, the majority of the test audience had trouble connecting to her. Although I felt she was great, the decision wasn't left to me. The design spot had an opening. I knew of just the right person for the position. I tossed my friend and former *Trading Space*'s designer, Lauren Makk's name into the hat. Lauren auditioned and landed the job. I was thrilled to be working with her again.

You know when you meet someone, and things just click and all of a sudden you are lifelong best friends? Well, that's Lauren and me. As she always said on *Trading Spaces*, we are like peanut butter and jelly, nothing can separate us.

As the negotiations were underway, I started to really understand and appreciate the silver tray in which I was being served from while working on *Trading Spaces*. Truthfully, I was naïve. I had little understanding, at first, of how the world of television really worked. *Trading Spaces* was established. It had the budget and amenities of a number one rated show. I took every single aspect, whether flying first class or staying in the finest hotels, for granted. I simply had no idea.

At least not until the new show began. With everything, you must build a following. New shows generally do not have a following regardless of the cast. That also means everything is done on limited funds and amenities. We would have to prove ourselves and build up to the magnitude *Trading Spaces* had become. The higher the demand and the viewing numbers the more commercial space was worth. That is how *Trading Spaces* was able to offer us "champagne wishes and caviar dreams" as they used to say on the show *The Lifestyles of the Rich and Famous*. I quickly learned to kiss fancy hotel rooms, rental cars, and caviar goodbye.

Not only that, I could kiss the handsome payment I received per episode while only working two days on set goodbye too. Here I would work for less and three times as hard. We were left to pay for our own living accommodations and had no rental car. It was eye-opening, and yet, this was the price of fame.

I am only telling you this part because it was the first time I realized how good I had it before. I had a new respect for budgets, audiences, and advertisers. With the silver tray now being replaced with a paper towel, a shoestring budget, more complications arose. I felt we were misleading our audience.

It's called the magic of television for a reason. With the donations from vendors and outside companies that wanted exposure for their tile, sinks, toilets, you name it, the amount being spent on the remodels was adding up to be three or four times the amount of money we were leading our viewers to believe we spent. This didn't sit well with me. I hated misleading the people at home to think it is possible they could work in their own home on these smaller budgets with the same results. It simply wasn't the truth. While this is the norm for many shows, this wasn't how *Trading Spaces* worked.

The budget was one thousand dollars per household on *Trading Spaces*. If one cent was spent over that allotment, the designer would have to return something to get them back under budget. The integrity of this process was upheld on each and every episode. Everyone knew it and we held true to the premise of the show.

With that idea in my back pocket, the integrity of the new show soon became the next issue I would face. There was an episode where my personal and professional integrity was challenged. I may not have made every correct decision in life, but when it comes down to someone's health and well-being there is no wiggle room in my mind.

Soon after filming a segment on lead poisoning in a home, we found ourselves eradicating mold from a basement in order to turn it into a beautiful addition. Within the basement, there was one particular brick support pillar that was covered in white paint that dated back over fifty years. They wanted to take the paint off to restore the original brick. As the sanders and grinders hit the pillars;

red flags went up. I immediately said we had to stop and test the paint. With the paint being so old, there was a very good chance that it contained lead which was the very disaster we addressed earlier. With each layer that was sanded away, we were spreading it throughout the house. The ventilation system was uncovered and at this point, the dust was settling upstairs.

Although little things kept popping up, small warning signs continued to pop up that begged me to question my opportunity on the show. Nonetheless I stayed humbled and grateful to have an audience. I moved forward regardless of the warnings being raised before my eyes. I wanted and needed to keep the promise I made to God. I would continue on with this calling, and I would not back down.

As time ticked away and filming continued, I grew more and more unhappy. It's when I realized not everything we do in life will be a blockbuster, nor will it be as sweet as peach cobbler. It kept me humble. It also helped that God kept reminding me I was there for a purpose.

Let me be clear, the network I was working for had nothing to do with my experiences on this particular show. Production companies are different than the network airing the show. I am simply relaying my experiences. I have no interest in insulting or slandering anyone. I'll say things weren't always bad. Those were just a few instances that can honestly happen to anyone with or without a television camera pointing at you. It's just one that you must take care of properly should it occur. There were moments where I was humbled to be God's servant too.

One of our homes was in massive disrepair. It was a beautiful place with plenty of potential. The problem was the homeowner became accustomed to living in a state of chaos. It happens in every city across the country, more often than one would think. We were there to help finish what had been started. The homeowner was a single mom with a son who was about to graduate. She wanted to finish the house before he graduated high school and left for college.

The pair had been battling issues for quite some time. Mom wanted to hold on to the last few days she had with her son around, and he wanted some space. She was strict, and honestly, he needed that. Just as the temple is the reflection of what is going on in the inside, so too is the home. Things weren't stellar.

I'm not sure what it is about my southern drawl or offering up advice with a dash of southern persuasion, but it relaxes people and soothes their discomfort. The walls and barriers we place around ourselves fall away. While we were working away, I was able to grab on and pull him in. We did a lot more than just rehabbing a home during our week with this family. We were able to rehab a relationship. I had learned from my father's passing that no one would want ever to leave this earth with a broken bond, especially that of a mother and son.

If I touched only two lives during this show, I'm glad it was theirs. It taught me we all had experiences, ups and downs, because it may be that someone else needs us in that place with them, even if it is even for a moment.

Before the season ended, I knew I wanted to make a change. I would not renew my contract if the offer came. I found myself complaining more than enjoying my time on television. Sure, it wasn't *Trading Spaces* but it was a paying job that kept me relevant. As it turned out, the show was canceled.

When it wrapped, I was out of a television job. I would go back to North Carolina and pick up my business where I had left off. God has a funny way of grasping me, shaking my shoulders, and knocking me over the head.

Hundreds of shows didn't make it in the wake, though. I'm hopeful it will come. In these past years, I've honed my skills to a fine mastery. I've learned a thing or two about life, and I've come to understand that you just have to keep going. With each day that passes, each new opportunity that comes my way, I look for the humble pie inside it knowing I will one day get that side of vanilla ice cream to go with it. Going from a silver tray to a paper towel builds character, develops humility, teaches respect, and requires hope to never give up and continue to climb.

Tools in the Toolbox
Tool #17: Humility

I can say without a doubt the tool of humility, with all it has to offer, has been the tool that has changed, helped, impacted, and improved my life the most. The antonym to conceit is humility. After all, I have spoken to you about understanding my greatest sin was my faith in myself. For years, I lived my life in a self-centered faith. The focus wasn't on God and His image, but it was simply on my own.

Having humility is a tough lesson at times. There are no perfect humans. God purposely made us flawed and vulnerable. When false attributes like pride and conceit fill our heads, we forget God wants our focus to be on Him. I lacked humility.

Humility is simply the act of being vulnerable. It's hard sometimes to let others see our mistakes, our flaws, the little things that make us tick, but it is necessary. There were times that I wasn't concerned with God's purpose for me, only my purpose.

I must say my faith in myself and perceived flaws were never used to intentionally hurt or harm others. In fact, it was the complete opposite. I have always had a heart that wants to serve others and help others to succeed. I took on roles such as chaplain, big brother, and LifeGroup leader not because I would benefit the most but I was pleasing God. It made me and those I surrounded myself with better people. That is the wonderful side of humility.

Now, think about the phrase "Step or think outside the box." When you step outside your comfort zone, the four lines you've drawn around yourself to protect your inner interest, you have created a vulnerable space. I spent years protecting myself by staying within the places I knew I could shine. I didn't put myself on the stage in college to star in the play because I didn't want to be seen in any light other than how I saw myself. Later, I never wanted to place myself in the eyes of casting directors if I knew there wasn't a chance I couldn't get the part. I wasn't humble enough to handle rejection. What happened when I let go of my selfish desires and was rejected? I was blessed with fulfilling my dreams.

A close friend recently told me, "Vulnerability is the new perfection." I love this saying.

The only way we can help ourselves is to be transparent about our journeys and our struggles. I want to be truly honest and say it has not been easy being so open and vulnerable with you.

Publishing my struggles and tragedies means wrestling with and laying down the worst parts of me. The parts that we all have but want to be kept in secret, whether we successfully hide them from the world or not. On the flipside, through this journey I have never felt more free or humble. This vulnerability has allowed me to know my storms have built my faith.

I tell people all the time, it's really too bad we all don't live the lives we see on our social media profiles. We would be surprised by the actual person behind the post.

They are flawed just like you and me. We all make mistakes. We all get down. We all have weaknesses.

Are you willing to admit that you are not perfect? Are you willing to show your biggest weakness?

Just like our other tools, you can practice humility. This is of paramount importance to deepen your relationship with God, those in your life, and the world itself.

While it's often difficult, accept your limitations. Not everyone possesses every talent, trait, and physical ability.

While you are accepting your own limitations, learn to accept others for theirs too. It's humbling to know we cannot expect everyone to be the person we are. This is a very freeing element in life.

Recognize your own faults. This is a tough one, but it is necessary if you want to live a faithful and rewarding existence.

Don't be afraid to make mistakes. Mistakes are the education we need to push us forward. Think about how I learned that I needed to glue pieces of wood together instead of simply nailing the pieces I used. If I didn't make that mistake I would probably still be missing the glue.

Carry an attitude of gratitude.

Most importantly, remember the only way to understand humility is to be humble. It's a practice, an art, a highly important life skill.

If you are ready to see life open up in a new way, if you are ready to humbly welcome inner peace and life without reservations, I offer you tool #17, Humility. It's time to grab a slice of humble pie. Go ahead, enjoy it, because once you taste it, you'll realize how good it really is.

Toss this tool in the box and come along.

Chapter 19
Would You Like Seconds With a Side of Patience?
"Now glory be to God, by his mighty power at work within us is able to do far more than we would ever dare to ask or even dream of—infinitely beyond our highest prayers, desires, thoughts or hopes."
Ephesians 3:20

Time and perspective have a way of showing you the meaning of gratitude and a deeper level of patience. These last few years have taught me more than many of my years combined. You ease into your age. You get to know yourself and find a balance that cannot be easily found in our younger years. You learn what value is and where it should be placed. It's a welcomed and exquisite place in my opinion.

While I've found myself waiting for the next big television opportunity to come, I've realized that God has only been strengthening my foundation. When this book was first presented to me, the idea of helping others was intriguing. Little did I know that this journey would heal me too. Writing your life story isn't easy. It begs you to dig deeper into the person you are behind the outer exterior. It asks you to cry a bit, laugh more than you ever thought possible, and to slow down. It makes you take it easy and realize how blessed life has been. This has been a tremendous, humbling, satisfying, and at times, out of control experience. Within it all, I believe God has been testing my readiness for the next big adventure he has on the horizon.

When we came to the table to write, one of the things we discussed was what I'm doing now. It was mentioned that people would find that as interesting as where I've been and what I've done in the past. Well, honestly, I've been learning, growing, educating myself, and building faith.

As my last show came to an end, I didn't realize that would be it for a while. Things moved so quickly after *Trading Spaces* ended I figured the next go around would be no different. I was wrong. I took it all for granted. I laugh at my unhappiness now. I was displeased with my last show because it wasn't what I had previously. Now, I think of it as something I had and isn't that better than nothing? Again, age and perspective are a beautiful thing.

While I've been diligently pursuing the next show, there have been many other opportunities offered. Living in North Carolina proved to be difficult at first, due to not being in the epicenter for television or modeling such as L.A. or New York, but with the availability of modern technology, I have been able to interview when my name is selected. You may be asking if I've been called, why am I currently not on television? It's not that I'm not grateful for the opportunities that have been presented because I am wholeheartedly thankful, but in the television industry, the contractual obligations and terms are sometimes not in my best interest. Either the show is across the country and will not pay for living expenses, or travel is not covered, the time commitments are unreasonable, or even the payment per episode doesn't match the time allotted for the show's production. Like my *Trading Spaces* co-star Lauren says, "If it ain't rats, it's roaches." I laugh every time I say it. It's the truth in life. If it ain't one thing, it's another.

I've lived long enough to know nothing will ever be perfect, but this next step in my life has to ignite my heart, put a skip in my step, and create a buzz inside my chest, all the things I was talking about before. It's got to *feel* like I did inside King's Custom Glass Company—world changing. I have to live by my own advice that I challenged you to, and do something I love so that I feel I never had to work a day in my life again. I had that once; I'll have it again.

The television world is funny. There is an aura around it that makes people question your career choices in a different way. One of the hardest and humbling questions I get often is: Do you have a new show yet? I say the hardest and humbling because it reminds me that I must keep persevering until the right prospect comes.

I would be lying if I don't tell you I laugh to myself and think, no not yet, but thanks for reminding me I don't have one yet. How many people ask the dentist, "So, did you pull any teeth today?"

Or even the auto mechanic, "So tell me, what are your chances for changing the oil in a car tomorrow?"

This is their daily life. My job and its processes are mine. It's funny how some fields have a double standard. When I was modeling full-time, I was questioned about landing the cover, not just the inside pages. I suppose, in the end, it's all relative. The truth is, when I'm asked if I've landed the next gig, I hate saying no, not yet, it will come, I'm still holding out because it does sting. This is my life's passion; I want it so badly because it is my true calling. Patience and perseverance are my key to holding steady in God's calling for me. I've been humbled. I've learned. I'm ready.

I recently wrote and shot what is called a sizzle reel. That's a short video that pitches a show idea, and its host. Working with the ideas that are popular today, flipping houses, downsizing, and repurposing, I put a whole new twist to a unique show idea. The pitch is currently with production companies awaiting an answer. Several have liked it, but no deal has been inked as of yet. My hopes are lifted; my perseverance is strong. I yearn to continue this journey in my life. It's the passion that sets my soul ablaze.

Many may ask about modeling. I cannot help but smile at those days. I learned so much when I traveled. It opened my eyes to the ways of the world, the different cultures available to all of us, and the miraculous wonders God created. My days of gracing the pages of Men's Health and W Magazine are somewhat in the past. My focus has been more geared to television, however one of the things still I treasure are the ten to twelve runway charity shows I do each and every year. Not only are they rewarding, they humble me and make me beyond grateful for the life God has provided. That is not to say that if I were called to do another campaign, I wouldn't consider the offer. I would.

It's just not my everyday life right now.

What is my everyday life is my business, Homecierge. Being able to tap into the creativity that I first discovered in Kindergarten is rewarding. There is no better feeling than creating a unique, new space in someone's home that you know they will treasure for years to come whether it's a new kitchen, a downstairs Irish pub, a custom wooden desk or the hottest new trend of live edge wood tables, or even an insane treehouse. Each project is unique and satisfying. I love the looks on homeowners' faces when they have seen their dreams come true. It's amazing to see your artwork hanging in the coolest hotspots in town. I realize how fortunate God's vision and path is for me. Not everyone gets to do what they love the most.

Through everything there is one simple fact that I most want everyone to know; I'm a normal guy. I'm a guy who works on deadlines. Struggles. A man who finds himself in everyday situations. A guy whose dreams are so big only God can make them happen. I believe in the future, in building faith, in purpose and a plan. I believe that no matter what I've walked, God hasn't even begun to scratch the surface of what He has in store for me. Isn't that an amazing thought?

In the meantime, I continue to hone my craft patiently. I used to say I'm a jack of all trades and a master of none. Now I like to say, I'm a jack of all trades and a master of many, but I will never say all because no one is above learning a little more or something new. I open my eyes each day with knowledge that I'm blessed. I continue to strive forward, to educate myself, be diligent and persevere. One of my favorite quotes is an old Indian Proverb: "When you were born, you cried, and the world rejoiced. Live your life in such a way that when you die, the world cries and you rejoice."

This sums up my life every day. I entered into the world fresh and new, shed some tears, experienced some highs and lows, but those who were, and still are my world, were happy I arrived. My goal and purpose are to fill the hearts and share my passion for improving each life I'm so fortunate to be touched by and that I have touched. This is my way of showing God that I am the church. When it's my time to leave this earth, I hope that I have left it a better place.

Tools in the Toolbox
Tool #18: Perseverance

"You may encounter many defeats, but you must not be defeated. In fact, it may be necessary to encounter the defeats, so you can know who you are, what you can rise from, how you can still come out of it."
Maya Angelou

You know by now life is never a straight and narrow path. It's fraught with bends, twists, and upheavals. Each obstacle that arises ushers in a new life lesson. You have two choices when you find life in this state: give up or persevere. Giving up is generally easier, but being able to persevere offers so much more in the end.

Perseverance is the ability to keep going, to keep trying, no matter what life throws your way or how many times your attempts may fail. There is a reason why I saved this tool until this point. Your arsenal of tools already includes acceptance, diligence, patience, listening, and humility. Until you have mastered these tools, staying on a positive and steady course is often extremely trying.

Learning to master the art of perseverance means you keep trying at all costs. That doesn't mean that every situation will work out the way you want each and every time. It simply means you have a healthy attitude towards success. It's through persistence that we create an inner strength that pushes us forward.

I have experienced many ups and downs. I have come through each of these moments in hopes to one day be

269

blessed with another ability to transform, reach, and build others up with positive reinforcement. If I had given up on my dreams after my shows were wrapped, I wouldn't have been given these moments with you. My ultimate goal of reaching people and building faith would have fallen by the wayside. That seems worse to me than any issue I would have or still have to brave. This drive and perseverance also lets me know that God is not holding me back, but instead preparing me for more opportunities that He has lying in wait over the horizon.

When life gets hard and quitting seems easier, try this approach: Accept the situation. Be realistic about where you are. Is this truly temporary even if it feels like forever? While you are accepting the situation, be patient in understanding how and why you must handle it with the utmost perseverance.

Be diligent. Never let your head tell your heart that persevering through the problem is impossible. Nothing is impossible.

Listen to God's word and be humbled by the chance to overcome, gain strength, and carry on in true perseverance.

Purposely try something you have failed doing before. You have the power and ability to succeed no matter how many tries it takes to get it right. This attitude breeds success.

What do your goals look like? Think about your long-term and short-term goals. Are they obtainable? If not, pare them down. Obtainable goals, no matter how difficult the plan, create a workable and persevering plan.

Stay positive.

Start out small and work your way to brighter and better days.

Perseverance is a characteristic each of us should embrace. I've always said, "Dream so big only God can do it." I adapted that from the Jackie Paulson quote, "Dream so big only God can fulfill it." The longer you work towards your goals, the bigger the blessings that will come.

Have faith. Move forward in God's plan for you. Be perseverant.

If you are willing to give life all you've got, you have tool #18, Perseverance. Toss it in your toolbox and come along.

Chapter 20
Your Blueprints Are Ready

Your blueprints are ready. The pages are outlined and perfectly dotted with the instructions for building your best life. While you are now holding all the building tools, I must ask if your foundation has properly set.

That foundation started when I told you in the very beginning: I am the church. I will repeat that *I am the church*. I am a Christian. These are the two most powerful descriptions and fundamentals of who I am. I do not solely define myself with the word model. Nor is it by the word celebrity. It's not even the word carpenter. I'm Brandon. I am the church. I am a Christian; that is the man, the foundation of who I am.

Throughout this amazing journey of my life's experiences, I've given you the tools of the toolbox which I've built, grown to know, and use in my daily life. While these instruments are so very important, they can only be used if started with the proper relationship with God. This relationship is of greater importance than asking yourself a few questions and checking a mental box of whether you have or are able to apply these tools of life. In fact, the tools are only helpful if they are used with the steady foundation of faith. It's the means by which you build faith and that relationship with our maker. When building, all blueprints cannot be built until they are stamped by an Architect. You must get the stamp from the Architect of life, our Heavenly Father.

The most powerful advice I can give to you is to move away from the idea that church is a specific location only. It's not just a building to pass through every Sunday or for some the place to avoid. It should be less of a ritual and more about a relationship, not only with God but also with yourself. When Christians move from the walls of the church building, resting on a solid foundation, and actively engage those around them by showing the lessons we learn throughout all aspects of life, that is when the walls fall away, and you *ARE* the church. Jesus didn't say watch me and I will show you how to fish; he said, let me teach you and you will never go hungry. Be the church and your foundation will never break. It may shake, but it will always right itself when God is in the lead. This, my friends, is how you build faith through your hands, as I have built mine through my carpenter's hands.

I think about the power of the bulldozer sinking when I was a child. Everything changed. A course and direction that my parents planned were disrupted and recalculated. New blueprints were drawn for a life that leads each of us down a more focused and solid path. The sinkholes in life are designed to educate you on the importance of wisely choosing solid ground to pour your foundation upon.

My message throughout this book in regards to faith is simply this: faith is a decision to trust. It's a decision to believe. The way God knows you have expressed your understanding of faith is through the power of surrender. We are tempted to put our faith in many things. Some people put all their faith in God and lead a righteous life.

Others put it in their money, themselves, their friends, or their surroundings. Some split their beliefs while keeping God and faith in equal proportion. Our choices as to where we place our faith seem endless these days, but if we come to understand what God is all about, our faith grows. Where does your faith lie?

This great life that I keep asking you to live doesn't happen by accident. It's the result of putting the tools in the toolbox into action. It's about removing the situations that continually set you up for stress and failure. Start setting yourself up for a life of love, success, creativity, passion, faith, and blessings.

You must do so by customizing the tools to fit your own needs and lifestyle while keeping them centered in a foundation of faith. Think about the way the tools all work together.

First, you come to know faith in God, then yourself. Then you remove the barriers of only hearing the word of God and decide to become the word. You are now tasked with being the carpenter of your life. Once again, Maria Robinson says it best, "Nobody can go back and start a new beginning, but anyone can start today and make a new ending." Today is the day you have the ability to start over and create a new blueprint. Perhaps your overall plan is in pretty good shape, but it's time to add an addition. Maybe you're right where you need to be and these tools are nothing but solid reminders of living the life God has called you to lead. No matter where you are in life, your tools are ready.

Think of all the ways one tool helps another. Beginning with *Tool #1: Pouring the Footers,* we are called to remember this is *our* ground floor. The word "our" is italicized because I ask you to remember that my blueprint is uniquely mine. As yours are uniquely drawn for you. The beauty of the blueprint is we are all created to have our own set of circumstances, however, that doesn't mean that just because they are different we cannot come to learn the same lessons and harvest the same value out of each of these experiences. The most important part of pouring our footers is to remove the burdens of our lives so that our structure, that sound foundation, cannot fail. Without the proper foot placement, whether a house or your life, you'll never be able to withstand and hold up the goals and future you are being called to lead. I'll ask you for the last time, is your foundation solid?

If it is, pick up *Tool #2: Acceptance.* Your foundation is unshakeable, but have you built it in an acceptance of God? Remember there is a difference in knowing there is a higher power and truly knowing Him in your heart. Accepting God and asking for His forgiveness is actually acknowledging to Him that you are not perfect and you will make mistakes. Even the best blueprint can have design flaws.

This too is as much about personal acceptance as it is Godly acceptance. Speaking of personal acceptance, I must remind you that we are all different. Some want to be President. Some want to be firefighters. Some want to be stay-at-home parents. Some want to be television and movie stars. Some want to build a life around greatness, where some are happy living a normal existence. Whomever you are, whatever you long to be, I challenge you to accept that person. God never makes mistakes! Believe in God, accept God, believe in you, accept you, that is the only way the load-bearing walls of your blueprint can be properly constructed. Are you ready to live a life built around favorable approval?

If so, ***Tool #3: Caring for the Seed*** is ready to be drawn into the mix. Remember the parable of the mustard seed? It's the small seeds of life that grow into something mighty. God, whether through our hopes, desires, and inner callings or with people like Professor Pilkington, plant seeds of growth in our lives. These are the true details in which we create the design of our blueprint.

When we find passion for something we love, we develop roots. Just like a plant in your garden, after the seed is planted, it needs nutrients to fertilize your calling and water to help your purpose bloom. If you want inner and outer growth in all areas of your life, you must take time to flourish in your gifts and talents. You must take the time to water God's seeds. We do so by establishing a solid foundation, understanding and practicing acceptance, using our talents and callings to our best abilities, and even through planting our own seedlings. Without proper care, our seeds wither away. Allowing your purpose to remain unfulfilled leads to an unfilled life. Are you able to fabricate the blueprint God set out for you to design? Are you watering your seeds?

Tool #4: Pruning Shears are an essential tool to keep oiled and ready for use. Remember the quote by Eric Burdon, "Inside each of us, there is a seed of both good and evil. It's a constant struggle as to which one will win." Sometimes our blueprints get out of whack. We draw a curve where a straight line is required to hold up the surrounding walls. Like in life, sometimes seeds are planted that do our foundation no justice. Even when planting grass seeds it is impossible to remove seeds that grow weeds.

When things start to grow in our lives that are not worthy of living as God has set forth for us, we must use our shears to remove these seedlings fostering the growth of negativity within our lives. If left unattended those seeds become the weeds that will choke the seedlings of their purity. Ivy may look appealing as it grows around the base of a tree, but over time it chokes the tree. Once it has completely engulfed it, it slowly steals the nutrients and leaves nothing but a rotten trunk within. We must prune the harmful weeds and ivy in our life so that we may continue to reach and climb towards the light above.

Remember those sucker limbs we spoke of? You've come too far in life to let wild branches take over. These are the branches of over indulgence and taking advantage of your blessings. You must prune them and not allow them to divert attention to greed and ungrateful direction in your growth. Maintain, prune, and remove what is not worthy of the blueprint God set forth for your life.

No person can truly flourish if they are missing ***Tool #5: Believe in Yourself***. Each of our blueprints was created in God's image. We are perfect. We are beautiful. You must always believe you have the power to create, to build, to live what was created for you. If you stand firm in your beliefs both spiritually and mentally, no one can break down the walls you have created nor shake your foundation. Each of us is given a moral compass to help build this belief. I ask that you never allow that compass to be affected by the magnetic charge of temptation, pain, greed, or upset to pull you away from your original construction. Remember the beliefs you hold dearest are shown in all you do and, in the end, you are rewarded with immeasurable blessings if you believe in yourself because of your belief in God. Are you standing in His image? Start with what is within and then project your brilliance outward unto the world. It's the only way your blueprint will also have desirable curb appeal.

Tool #6: Judgment and Forgiveness can affect our overall blueprint more than just about any other tool. We must learn to live a life as free of judgments as possible. One book cover may not be as appealing to you as the other, but you never know which is the most interesting until you open it up and begin to read what lies within the pages. When we prejudge and live by preconceived notions only, we strip ourselves from the pleasures of experiencing something beautiful God had in store for us. In terms of forgiveness, while it can be a tough tool to practice and apply in our lives, it is so very necessary that we give this gift to others as much as we give it to ourselves. We are all flawed, period, no exceptions. We all make mistakes in making snap judgments and sometimes irresponsible decisions. In the end, our blueprint is so much better if we remove poor decisions and irresponsible judgments from our lives. Get to know the situation, the person, the possibility before you suggest a change. If you find yourself falling into this trap or someone places these standards upon you, take a step back, forgive, and continue to build your blueprint in His image.

Building takes time. ***Tool #7: All in God's Timing*** reminds us that even if our blueprint doesn't come together in one smooth transaction, the design will come when or if it is destined to be. Timing is truly everything in life. Remember that rejection is God's protection. If you don't see your dreams coming to flourish the way you would like, ask yourself, what is God protecting me from?

God knows what is over the horizon. He knows when your blueprint needs to be tweaked.

I cannot tell you how many times I've had to tweak my plans. It's when we redirect and redesign our plans that a greater outcome is revealed. Are you willing to give up the control, worry, and doubt of trying to force everything into your timeframe? God's plan is so much better than our own. We must surrender our own ideas and take security in knowing that God has us right where we need to be at any given time.

That leads us to apply ***Tool #8: Knowing Your Place*** to our overall blueprint. This one is sometimes hard to exercise in life. The basic idea can go two ways, both positive and negative. When situations come up ask yourself these basic questions: Will my presence help the situation? Is it healthy for me to be involved? Is this my place? Does the situation warrant my help? If you are able to answer yes then you know God is calling you to this place. If the answer is no and you feel moved to step forward regardless, do your best to really think about the end result. What is really motivating you forward? Why do you feel this is your place? Not every blueprint needs multiple levels when it's drawn, so don't feel forced to add in features and situations where they are not needed. Stay within your budget, per se. Never write a check you cannot cash.

When crafting the best design for our lives, we must use ***Tool #9: Diligence***. Do you remember the definition of diligence? It's the careful and persistent effort towards the work you are being called to do. God asks us to be diligent in our passion for him. He asks us to do the same when it comes to spreading His word and living in His image. If you apply diligence to your blueprint and to the practice of all the other tools I've handed to you, then you will be pleasing in the eyes of God. This is one of the highest honors to possess in your character. Are there places you are lacking this essential tool? Could you be more diligent in your faith? If you faithfully build this into everything you do and create, it will foster an award-winning life.

Tool #10: Patience asks that we act in moral excellence with an even-temper and steady perseverance. This is the tool that requires you to cultivate over time. Remember if you "Take it easy. Take it slow, but always stay ahead" in all that you do in life, patience comes. We must be patient, savor the moments of our life, and appreciate the blueprint coming together. This is how we create balance in our life. Without patience, we lose our ability to see the events that open bigger doors and greater blessings.

I'll admit God was extremely patient with me when he tossed *Tool #11: Surrendering* in my toolbox. He asked me to give up control so many times, as I'm sure He has done to you. Moments where we are asked to give up control come within a small test or the massive upheavals that shake our foundations. Each one of these experiences is designed to beg us to surrender to His will. It's sometimes hard to give up control, but what we must focus on is what will come once we do. There is always something bigger to add to the blueprint if you are willing to surrender.

On the other hand, God asks of us to never surrender our morals or our beliefs. Instead He asks us to learn, to grow, to expand our horizons, and do so on the foundation He gave us to build upon. Sometimes surrendering is needed every single day. Sometimes it is more of a moment in life. But regardless when those times come, it's important to remember what God is calling us to do—turn over our desires and allow Him to help in all that we do. Have you fully surrendered?

Without *Tool #12: Temple*, we cannot have a blueprint. Remember what I said, your temple is your toolbox. This is the place we must keep the spirit of patience, acceptance, belief, and faith inside. Again, the body, your temple, is magnificent in all its glory. It's our greatest gift. God calls us to use it wisely, take care of, and use it to model and shine in His word. It's in our human nature to gravitate towards people with like minds. If we are being the church and building faith, we will seek those who use their temples in the same manner. We also move towards those we most admire and want to model our lives after. If we stand firm in faith, our temples show we are using our tools of life to live in God's blueprint. By neglecting this powerful gift God gave us, whether physically or emotionally, we are ignoring God's calling. It takes time to organize the toolbox. It takes keeping our temple healthy in His spirit to fully execute what God has for us. If you allow God's spirit to pour over you, your soul and plans will be oiled. This is the tool that is the most precious.

God is selfless. He gave each of us a unique design in order to learn ***Tool #13: The Art of Blessing.*** The number one way to craft your blueprint in such a way that it will always be successful is to bless others and never expect something in return. As God gives us gifts of life, relationships, our needs met, and so much more, He also asks us to complete the circle. We are here to give of ourselves. Remember that blessings do not have to be in the material form. They can come in the gift of love, respect, friendship, or even a hello and a smiling face when the world feels upside down. Approach your life selflessly. This cultivates the art of blessing others without even trying. If you are being called to bless someone, ask yourself why? Is God telling you to give? My mother never wanted anything in return for her work with the hospice care center. But the spoils of her blessing came in the peace my father had when he passed. Blessings big and small make our world a much better place. Every day ask yourself, have I been a blessing? Each blessing only strengthens our foundation tenfold.

When we live a blessing-giving and -filling life we create and use *Tool #14: Empathy.* Empathy is the tool we use to break down the barriers that form around our temples and blueprints in order to keep the outside world at bay. Empathy is when we feel with a person or a situation. Empathy is the glue that connects our souls. It's the place that teaches us we are not alone in this world. It allows us to have emotional connections. We have to give of ourselves in order to know what someone else is going through. We have to be able to listen, be courageous, and active in our lives and others' in order to understand and be empathetic. I asked you before and I'll ask you again, do you have the ability to see the world the way someone else does? Do you give of yourself? Do you use the power God gave each of us to connect with those around you? It's amazing what happens when you drop your walls and allow not only God but others inside your life.

Speaking of listening, *Tool #15: Listening* is so very important. If we do not listen how will we know when we need to make changes to our blueprint? This is the tool that you can never use too much. I spoke about the art of listening when it comes to prayer. So many go into prayer with requests, concerns, and needs, but do not take the time to actually listen for God's responses. A conversation can only be had if two parties are engaged. Do you listen? Do you take the time to hear God and all that He is doing for you? Not every life-changing communication whether from above or here on earth comes when life is hard. God and those around you know if you are listening. They see it in your actions. So I ask you: are you a listener or a speaker? I dare you to create balance.

Tool #16: Purpose and Calling all comes to pass when you use all these tools at once. We all have a purpose. This is why we have a working blueprint. We have a designed purpose that God has so graciously placed us on this earth to fulfill. The calling waiting for you should create an inner feeling that gives you an extra skip in your step, makes your heartbeat quicken, and pushes your head higher in the air because you know you are doing God's work. Remember when I said, "If you love what you do, you'll never work a day in your life?" It's so true. If you follow your purpose and answer God's call, work is never equated with your days. Instead you only have passion. Furthermore, we are here to share what God has given to us. Are you answering that call? Has your purpose been revealed? If not, don't worry, it will come. But once it does you must make yourself and God a promise. You must use your purpose to live life to the fullest.

While we strive to put all the tools into action and do so in the best form of God's image, we must use *Tool #17:*

Humility. Humility once again is nothing more than being vulnerable. When you step outside of the box, so to speak, you create vulnerable space. Humbling ourselves allows us to understand rejection. It helps us connect with others and practice humility. We all have weaknesses. We have to be able to allow ourselves to give grace to others when they are weak.

God does this for us. We must do it for ourselves and others. This is of paramount importance in order to deepen our relationships with God, those in our lives, and our relationships with the world. The only way to understand humility is to be humble. By doing so we welcome a level of inner peace. We also learn to live a life without reservation. Are you humble in all you do? Do you keep yourself open and willing to step outside your comfort zone to learn and interact?

Humility is so very important. A mistake doesn't define you forever, it's a way to humbly accept life's lessons.

And it's those life lessons that require us to use *Tool #18: Perseverance* every single day of our lives. You know by now life is never a straight and narrow path. It's fraught with bends, twists, and upheavals. Each obstacle has been designed to provide us with a new life lesson. Giving up is sometimes the easiest option, but when you utilize perseverance in life it's truly what helps us finally put our blueprints into an active life. Every day you must get up, look at yourself in the mirror, smile, and decide no matter how tough the day may be before you that you have God on your side and that you will persevere through every challenge. Listen to God's word and be humble in the knowledge that nothing is impossible.

Perseverance is what pushes us further in life. Start small and work towards the brightest and better days of what God has on your horizon. The longer you work towards your goals, the bigger the blessings that will come.

You are unique in your design. You have your tools. You have your talents. You have faith. Most importantly, you have God! How can you lose? The answer is you can't.

As for me, I am continuing to build. I will continue to strengthen my foundation every day of my life until God calls me to be among the flowers in His garden. Each day I pack up my tools, I use them wisely, and I look at my hands. A carpenter's hands are often stained, a bit beat up and rough, but in the end they are powerful. They build what others have called them to do. They are used to serve. I pray that each day I use my hands to build faith not only in myself but in you. Because no matter what may come, our dreams, our calling, that little push is God's way of saying we are His.

I am His.

In closing, I am still in the process of mastering and collecting the many tools I shared with you. That is why we are here on this earth, to learn, to experience, to grow. There is plenty of room for more tools in my toolbox. I'm never above saying I do not have all the answers. The fact is I never will have all the answers. That is the beauty of our blueprints, of our design, of God's will for us, because life is designed where we never have to worry about knowing it all.

The words of this book are what I felt God called me to witness to you. These are the stories and memories of my life best told through my recollections. They are meant to enlighten and encourage your desire to reach your inner calling and purpose. I pray they help you *BE*lieve in *YOU*rself and find the perfect image of how and why you were created.

Are my words perfect? Maybe not, but that doesn't make them wrong. It makes them what God has placed on my heart. I ask that you take the tools and lessons I've learned and apply them in a way that makes your journey more fulfilling. I am so grateful and humbled to be walking in your journey with you. Together we are the church, so it's time to head out into the community and fix it forward.

As for me, as for my life, well, my toolbox is ready and my work is to be continued…

Colossians 3 (NIV)

Living as Those Made Alive in Christ

1 Since, then, you have been raised with Christ, set your hearts on things above, where Christ is, seated at the right hand of God. **2** Set your minds on things above, not on earthly things. **3** For you died, and your life is now hidden with Christ in God. **4** When Christ, who is your[a] life, appears, then you also will appear with him in glory.

5 Put to death, therefore, whatever belongs to your earthly nature: sexual immorality, impurity, lust, evil desires and greed, which is idolatry. **6** Because of these, the wrath of God is coming.[b] **7** You used to walk in these ways, in the life you once lived. **8** But now you must also rid yourselves of all such things as these: anger, rage, malice, slander, and filthy language from your lips. **9** Do not lie to each other, since you have taken off your old self with its practices **10** and have put on the new self, which is being renewed in knowledge in the image of its Creator. **11** Here there is no Gentile or Jew, circumcised or uncircumcised, barbarian, Scythian, slave or free, but Christ is all, and is in all.

12 Therefore, as God's chosen people, holy and dearly loved, clothe yourselves with compassion, kindness, humility, gentleness and patience. **13** Bear with each other and forgive one another if any of you has a grievance against someone. Forgive as the Lord forgave you. **14** And over all these virtues put on love, which binds them all together in perfect unity.

15 Let the peace of Christ rule in your hearts, since as members of one body you were called to peace. And be thankful. **16** Let the message of Christ dwell among you richly as you teach and admonish one another with all wisdom through psalms, hymns, and songs from the Spirit, singing to God with gratitude in your hearts. **17** And whatever you do, whether in word or deed, do it all in the name of the Lord Jesus, giving thanks to God the Father through him.

Acknowledgment

Writing a book has always been on the short list of achievements I would have liked to conquer in my life, but this is not the book I thought I would have written as my first. Without my amazing co-author Danielle A. Vann, this book would still be mere scribbles on pieces of paper and not be the book printed before you.

When writing such personal experiences—whether it be what makes me happy or angry, what has uplifted me—it takes extraordinary, unchained vulnerability. Especially with the knowledge that I am exposing to any and every one that chooses to read it what makes my heart race with excitement or what brings me to a lower state of mind.

When Danielle listened to my story and then together we were able to write it out as if it were me telling it effortlessly, without hesitation, I realized how rewarding this would be for my life. I am hopeful it is beneficial to yours. It is very daunting thinking you can't mess up and you have to get it perfect because this is my life and I don't want to tell it wrong. It was Danielle that was able to capture the moments of my triumphs and tragedies that were special to me in building the foundation on which I now stand.

I would also like to acknowledge all my family and friends that have been so instrumental in fabricating the safety net to always catch me if I fell, but most importantly giving me the security and faith to JUMP. If you are not willing to jump, you will never know if you can fly.

Author Bios
Brandon Russell

Brandon is best known for his roles on TLC's *Trading Spaces*, A&E's *Drill Team*, the *Today* show, *The View*, and numerous other television shows around the globe. He has been featured in *Elevate Magazine*, *Epicurean Magazine*, *Men's Health*, *W*, *Jezebel Atlanta Magazine*, to list a few. Brandon has graced the runways for Guess, Nautica, Phat Farm, Jeffery and Belk. Although all of these are accomplishments he is very proud of, they are not the only things he hopes to be known for.

As a dedicated volunteer to various charities, and builder of his own foundation, Fix it Forward, Brandon's mission is to teach both life and home skills that spark a change. His hope is that ministering his faith into everything he does will inspire others to find their true calling. Just like his father's tools did for him. Brandon owns his own business, Homecierge, based out of Charlotte, North Carolina, where he currently lives.

Danielle A. Vann

Danielle A. Vann lives to write. When she was small, she spent endless days writing and crafting wild characters. As Danielle grew, that love for writing sparked a career in journalism. She began her career as a scriptwriter and then moved into a flourishing career as a news reporter, investigative reporter, food reporter, and morning/evening news anchor. That career earned her an Associate Press Award.

She also served as a public relationships representive for a major metropolitian city near Houston, Texas. Danielle is also the author of ***Gracie Lou and The Bad Dream Eater*** and the Gracie Lou Series, ***The Whizbang Machine*** and the Whizbang Machine series, and the adorable children's book, ***The Very Tall Tale of Ranger, the Great Pyrenees, and his Adorable Friend, Miss Keys.***

To learn more, visit www.authordanielleavann.com